THE MATTHEW HAYDEN COOKBOOK 2

THE MATTHEW HAYDEN COOKBOOK

Delicious recipes and terrific yarns
from Australia's gourmet cricketer 2

ABC
Books

Contents

INTRODUCTION

If someone had said to me five years ago, 'Haydos, I reckon you're gonna write a couple of cookbooks,' my reply would certainly have been, 'Mate, you've got to be joking!'

It's no secret that I love my food, but testing recipes and writing down stories about my experiences is a different thing altogether. The truth is, however, I absolutely love writing and cooking. Come to think of it, I have done ever since I was a little boy. And it's got to the point now where I field more questions in sporting press conferences on cooking and any interesting 'titbits' than on how the willow will be, or was, swung. Bizarre? Yes. But it has provided such a profoundly interesting twist to my professional and personal life that I just have to pinch myself sometimes to see if it really is true!

Food, and my love of it, have been the classic 'door-openers' for me across the world. Sometimes, just having that tiny common thread is enough to build friendships with people from all walks of life. Other people's stories have always been a tremendous source of interest to me over the years, and sharing a meal is a great way to break down any barriers. And there is something else that inspires me, too, whether it's in the sporting arena or in the kitchen. Passion! If you're passionate about the things you do, it makes an incredible difference to your motivation and your enjoyment. So many people are passionate and knowledgeable and articulate about their food experiences these days that I can't help wondering if *food* has become the modern-day home *sport*! I hope that this book, in some way, will give you a few good coaching tips. And to those of you who reckon they are 'the hope of the hopeless', let me confidently say this: if a cricketer can cook, surely you can have a crack at it!

Have a go! Enjoy!

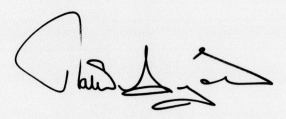

DOWN AND DIRTY IN DUNEDIN

Beautiful, proud Dunedin on the south-east coast of the southern island of New Zealand. It is home to thousands of tertiary students and, more than any other city in New Zealand, is built around great halls of learning. This injection of youth gives the place its own vibrant character, which the Australian cricket team experienced first-hand at a fast-food restaurant in the city.

We were playing a one-dayer against New Zealand, batted first and set a good total. They were defending very well and the exuberant crowd, comprising many young university students starved of international cricket, was obviously enjoying a great game, in more ways than one! Put night-time, excitement, youth and enthusiasm in a bowl, add a great game, stir in patriotism, leave for a while and then add heaps of alcohol, and you have a recipe for disaster. The crowd's behaviour was terrible!

I was fielding out on the boundary and cans of ale were getting pegged my way up to the time when Brett Lee hit New Zealand's favourite son, Adam Parore, in the head with a bouncer. The crowd went absolutely bozo! Play had to be stopped that evening for about 15 minutes and full cans of beer were removed from the ground. For our safety we had to congregate in the middle. It was disappointing, to say the least.

Anyway, we won the game — we smashed them! But afterwards there was no catering at the ground. No food! The boys were starving. Fast-food restaurants aren't my cup of tea, but beggars can't be choosers and there was nothing else open on our way back to the hotel. The boys piled into the restaurant and I was more than a little concerned, as there were lots of people inside.

We instantly attracted a lot of attention. Ricky Ponting and Adam Gilchrist walked in and word got around even before the rest of us entered that the Australian cricket team was right here in this restaurant! We might as well have had bullseyes on our backs.

The boys bought their food and we were ready to leave, but there's always one in a pack, isn't there? There was this bloke and I remember him well. He wore Adidas three-stripe track pants. He started hurling abuse at me and threw a few cheap shots my way. All I was interested in was getting the boys away from the restaurant and into the car, so I began back-pedalling, still facing the bloke, because I wasn't keen on getting a king hit from behind.

'Look, mate, I'm really not interested in fighting,' I said.

He kept on hurling abuse and pushed me.

Hoping to diffuse the situation, I said (counting to 10, I might add): 'OK. Look, mate … whatever!' I then closed the door and left.

'The crowd went absolutely bozo! For our own safety, we had to congregate in the middle of the ground'

In the morning, there were two Budget vans waiting to take us to the airport and there was a note with a knife plunged through it straight into one of the van's tyres. It read: 'HAYDEN! YOUR FAMILY WILL SUFFER', signed 'ADIDAS THREE STRIPES.'

The police moved in swiftly because of the insurance claim on the van. Then the New Zealand radio got involved. Australia's press, too, joined the party, and it unfurled into a big story.

As it turned out, the Dunedin people, being very proud of their sporting event, organised a phone-in to the radio station there. People were asked to give information about the malicious deed or the man responsible. There was so much public pressure that one week later, Adidas Three Stripes had to drag his sorry butt into the Dunedin police station to dob himself in!

That was a walk on the wild side in Dunedin, the city where integrity and pride lead the way and honesty, in the end, prevailed.

PRAWN RICE ROLLS

If you want to make these ahead of time, place in a single layer on a tray, cover with a damp cloth and place into the fridge.

2 large red chillies

2 tablespoons palm sugar

1 tablespoon fish sauce, approximately

1-2 tablespoons lime juice

1 medium carrot, cut into matchsticks

2 stalks celery, cut into thin strips

100 g snow peas, finely sliced

2 spring onions, finely sliced

1 cup (75g) bean sprouts

1 cup coriander leaves

15 x 22 cm round rice paper wrappers

15 large cooked prawns, peeled and halved
 lengthways

To make the dipping sauce, roast the chillies under a hot grill until the skin is black and blistered. Place into a plastic bag to cool then remove the skin and seeds. In a mortar and pestle, pound the chillies with the palm sugar. Add the fish sauce and lime juice, to taste.

Combine all the filling ingredients in a large bowl. Fill a shallow dish, large enough to hold a rice paper wrapper, with warm water. Working one at a time, dip a wrapper into the water and leave for about 1 minute, until soft. Drain, and place onto a clean tea towel.

Place a small handful of the filling across the base of the wrapper. Top with 2 prawn halves, then fold in the sides and roll up. Repeat with remaining wrappers and filling. Serve with the dipping sauce.

MAKES 15

FOOD FOR
THOUGHT

Kell

Grace

Josh

Idea

A couple of phone calls

Acceptances

Good recipes

Ingredients

The best produce

Creativity

Commitment

Pleasant work

Satisfaction

Preparation

Table décor

Presentation

The doorbell

Family

Friends

Fun

Laughter

Yarns

Mateship

Great food

Good wine

Relaxation

Reflection

Convivial atmosphere

Sounds of the ocean

Good attitude

Acceptance of the night

Wonderful memories

Memories that make up a lifetime

Life's story

The story is told

The story is retold

The story is passed down a generation

The story lives on

And on

And on

And on …

SANDCRAB LASAGNE

2 tablespoons olive oil

1 onion, finely chopped

2 garlic cloves, crushed

$^1/_4$ cup (60 ml) white wine

400g can diced Italian tomatoes

700 g bottle Italian tomato sauce (sugo)

1 teaspoon olive oil, extra

2 x 250 g packets instant lasagne sheets

200 g sandcrab meat

salt and pepper

1 cup (100 g) finely grated Parmesan cheese

$^3/_4$ cup (90 g) grated tasty cheese

$^2/_3$ cup (100 g) mozzarella cheese

$^3/_4$ cup (185 ml) pouring cream

Heat the oil in a large saucepan and cook the onion and garlic until soft and lightly browned. Add the white wine and then the tomatoes and tomato sauce. Simmer over low heat, partially covered, for 30 minutes.

Meanwhile, bring a large pot of salted water to the boil and add the extra olive oil. Add four lasagne sheets, one at a time, and cook for 5 minutes, until soft. Move them around with a fork while cooking to keep the sheets apart. Lift out with a large slotted spoon and plunge into cold water to stop the cooking process. Drain on a clean cotton tablecloth or tea towels.

Preheat the oven to 190C. Take the sauce from the heat. Add the sandcrab meat and fold through; season with salt and pepper. Combine the cheeses and cream in a separate bowl.

To assemble the lasagne, layer the pasta sheets and sandcrab sauce into a large (10 cup capacity) lasagne dish. Finish with a thin layer of sandcrab sauce then a topping of the cheese mixture. Bake for 30 minutes, until golden brown.

SERVES 6

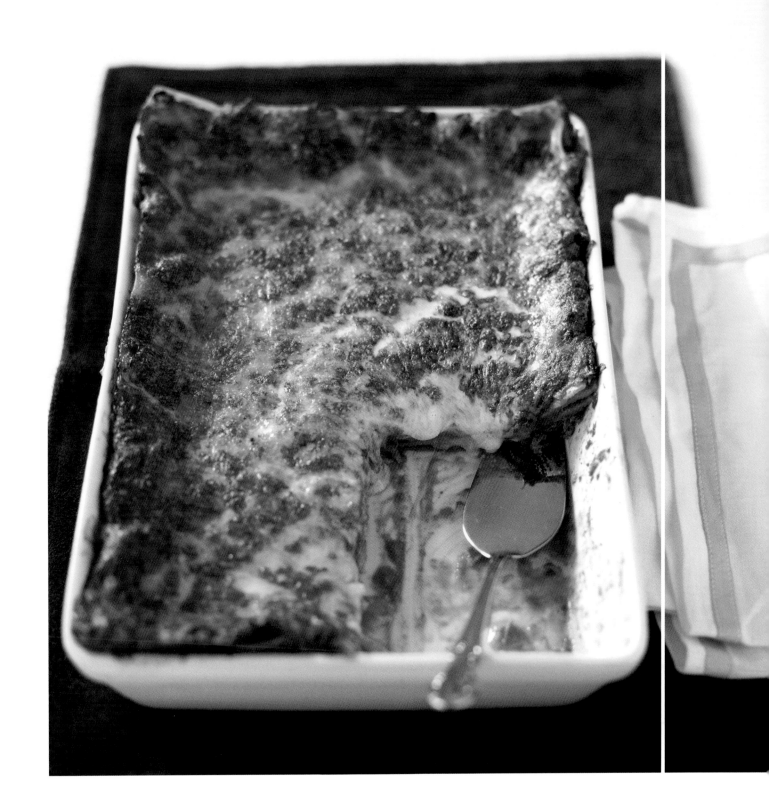

THE KING
AND I

I first met AJ when Jeff Thomson was coaching Queensland in 1991. He was invited to Queensland's cricket camp. I was a young bloke with the goal of playing for Australia, and like a moth to a naked flame is an ambitious sportsman drawn to the motivational words of Alan Jones. You can't help but be inspired by what he has to say, which, I guess, is why one in three people in Australia wakes up and listens to Alan Jones, 'The King' of early-morning talkback radio on Sydney's 2GB.

Alan was born in Oakey, in south-east Queensland. He has been adviser and speechwriter for former prime minister Malcolm Fraser, as well as senior English master at The King's School in Sydney. He has also been a very successful rugby coach, having masterminded the Wallabies' grand-slam tour in 1984. In 1985, he was named Australian coach of the year by the Confederation of Australian Sport

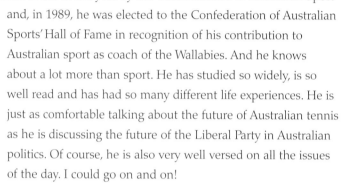

and, in 1989, he was elected to the Confederation of Australian Sports' Hall of Fame in recognition of his contribution to Australian sport as coach of the Wallabies. And he knows about a lot more than sport. He has studied so widely, is so well read and has had so many different life experiences. He is just as comfortable talking about the future of Australian tennis as he is discussing the future of the Liberal Party in Australian politics. Of course, he is also very well versed on all the issues of the day. I could go on and on!

What I really like about listening to AJ is that he cuts to the chase. He doesn't just waffle on but delivers his message succinctly, minus the icing sugar, in an easy-to-understand way. He is such a clear thinker and a superb entertainer. He has the ability, too, to make you feel good about yourself and to build your confidence. That's a wonderful gift, found in few people. He is blessed with so many strengths. To me, he has been an incredible role model.

There have been times in my life when I have clearly understood the Australian word 'mateship'. Alan calls it the Pick and Stick Club. That says it all in terms of his loyalty towards friends. He has always been a terrific supporter of mine, in good and bad times, the latter being when I found out who my true friends were.

Kell and I can certainly vouch for his extraordinary generosity, as well. It's a generosity that doesn't extend just to us but to many people in all walks of life. I remember being at Alan's home after one of Sydney's Test matches. Michael Bublé was playing on his stereo. I said, 'What a great voice. I really like listening to it.'

Alan said, 'Right.' He made a phone call and the next minute I was talking to Michael Bublé!

I believe the mark of a successful life is how many people you take along on the journey with you to share your success. That's the truly great part of being a cricketer because, in Australia and all around the world, there are millions of people being entertained at the one time. I never take that for granted. You know, the odd comment of 'Oh, I just loved that innings, mate', or 'We called our son Hayden after you', or 'Thanks for making my ill mum's life so happy. She just loves to watch you play', or 'Could you drop in to the hospital and see Joe when you get some time? A visit from you would really pick him up. You know, Matt, if you could only see his little face when they switch the TV on in hospital and he watches you bat! You're his hero!' That little face lives with me for a long, long time. I feel blessed to be able to make a difference. And Alan does that every time he speaks.

BUG TAILS WITH MANGO SALSA

This salsa is rich with the flavour of macadamias and mangoes, and adds a summery flavour to our most underrated crustacean – the Moreton Bay bug.

SALSA

2 large mangoes, diced
1 red onion, finely diced
1 red chilli, seeded and finely chopped
$\frac{1}{2}$ cup (70 g) crushed macadamias
$\frac{1}{2}$ cup coriander leaves, chopped
1 tablespoon olive oil
salt and pepper, to taste

1 cup (150 g) cornflour
500 g bug tail meat
1 cup (250 ml) vegetable oil

Combine all the salsa ingredients and set aside for the flavours to mingle.

Put the cornflour into a plastic bag, and add the bug tails. Twist the opening to seal, and shake to coat the tails. Heat the oil in a large wok. Shake off the excess cornflour, and cook the tails in 2-3 batches over high heat for 4-5 minutes, until lightly golden.

Drain on paper towels, and serve immediately with the mango salsa.

SERVES 4

THREE MEN AND A BOAT

Take a couple of good mates, a few willing (or not so willing) fish, some rods and bait – then add a boat. And there you have it – the perfect recipe for mateship.

When it comes to fishing expeditions I try to make sure I've got a few of my great mates on board, and Guy Reynolds and John Dumphy are perfect examples. We have had some great times together. You might remember them from my first book, where they got an honourable mention! Well, all of us lead pretty full-on lives – Guy runs the Macquarie Bank Sports Foundation (which I have been involved with for five years) and John is the boss of Shimano Fishing Industries in Australasia – so on the rare occasions when we manage to get together to indulge our passion for fishing, that time is golden.

Our adventures always reel in a good fishing story or two – so I've always got some yarns up my sleeve. On one particular expedition, we'd arranged to meet in Coffs Harbour, a great little coastal town on the east coast of Australia. In a lot of ways, it's really one of those 'last frontiers'. Even though it has developed enormously and rapidly, it is still very quiet and relaxing. A little ripper of a place! The perfect rendezvous for an unforgettable fishing expedition with some good friends.

The other reason we were all meeting in Coffs was because John was there with his massive fishing boat to compete in the Coffs Harbour fishing competition. Now, believe you me, John's boat was not any old boat. It was Shimano's number one game-fishing boat, which is set up for trolling lures around and catching marlin and whatnot. It goes all over the country. We'd decided it was an opportunity not to be missed. We could catch up and take advantage of the extraordinary snapper grounds that are second to none – only a couple of kilometres off-shore, they are simply astonishing and the stuff of legend!

Once we headed out to meet the fish, it was game on! You don't get three competitive blokes together and expect them to behave! We ribbed each other about everything under the sun – and especially our various fishing techniques! Being in a boat, as well, is the best. Especially a big one! And it's always great to get out to the sea, in it, on it and around it. I love it.

As a bonus, two of the day's prized fish were a pearled perch and a 7.5-kilogram snapper that I caught. I'd love to say it … I will say it! Of course, I out-fished them all! (It's my book, I can say what I like!) That night, we took the fish to a Thai restaurant, where they cooked up the most incredible scored and wok-fried snapper and pearly perch. Delicious!

We are so lucky to have such great-quality seafood in Australia, and there's something satisfyingly primal about catching your own fish. What a great feeling, being able to do that and literally put food on the table. Just magnificent!

The banter John, Guy and I share between fish and the swells is what keeps our friendship going – even if we don't see each other for a year or more, on our next fishing adventures we can always pick up where we left off. Fishing trips like this, and many others, always provide a welcome break for me. The demands of training and touring can make it hard for you to pursue your passions outside cricket – free time is hard to come by.

'There's something satisfyingly primal about catching your own fish'

23

WHOLE FRIED FISH WITH TWO SAUCES

I love this fish. It has lots of texture, with the crisp skin and
succulent moist white flesh around the bones. Yum!

4 x 600 g snapper or pearl perch, cleaned and
    scaled
1 bunch rosemary
2 cups (500 ml) olive oil
1 cup (150 g) cornflour
1 whole head garlic, broken into cloves and
    peeled

BALSAMIC SAUCE

¹/₂ cup (125 ml) balsamic vinegar
¹/₃ cup (80 ml) lemon juice

YOGHURT SAUCE

1 cup (250 g) plain yoghurt
2 tablespoons lime juice
¹/₂ cup coriander leaves
1 green chilli, seeded and finely chopped
salt and pepper to taste

Heat the oil in a large wok or heavy based frying pan until very
hot. Add the rosemary and garlic. Cook for 1 minute, then
remove and set aside. Working one at a time, dust the fish in
cornflour and shake off the excess. Cook the fish for 4 minutes
each side, until golden brown. Drain on paper towel. Repeat with
remaining fish, reheating the oil each time. Serve with one or
both of the sauces.

To make the balsamic sauce, place the reserved rosemary and
garlic into a medium saucepan. Add the balsamic vinegar, bring
to the boil and cook for 5 minutes, until reduced slightly. Stir in
the lemon juice, and pour into individual bowls for dipping.

To make the yoghurt sauce, place all the ingredients into a food
processor and process until smooth.

SERVES 4

GREEN AND GOLD ALL ROUND

It was the second Test match, Australia versus West Indies, and a very significant one at that. I was as happy as a pig in mud since I had a front-row seat to watch Michael Hussey reach his potential on the international stage. Together, Michael and I were involved in a wonderful partnership, every batsman's dream, culminating in not only both of us making hundreds but also leading the charge in our crushing victory over the West Indies. Party time! And when Australia wins a Test match in under three days, the days off are gold – and in this case, they were 'green and gold'!

We don't always hang out together on these days off but, in true Aussie spirit, we had organised to come together that evening to watch Australia's play-off match against Uruguay to qualify for the World Cup finals.

The tasks of the day were set out: Andrew Symonds (Simmo) and Michael Clarke (Pup) were to go fishing and catch flathead (they actually did it this time too!). Ricky Ponting and I were responsible for getting other odds and ends, and bought some fresh blue-eye trevalla and scallops from the beautiful little seafood markets nestled along Hobart's picturesque waterfront. And Stuart MacGill, aptly nicknamed Grape Juice, and Adam Gilchrist (Gilly) were sent on a mission to unveil Tassie's finest pinot noir.

Now, on most footy nights, an unusual tension exists. Pup, Simmo and I love rugby league, in line with the east coast tradition. Ricky is an AFL man, Tassie born and bred, and Gilly is our number one soccer fan. But on this night differences were cast aside as we'd had a solid dose of patriotism firmly injected into our veins after our demolition of the WI and, enthusiastically and excitedly, we came together as one to watch history in the making. Go Australia! Go! Sweet victory again! You beauty! Australia was off to the World Cup in Germany.

I reckon that night we had the recipe for green and gold success – great mateship, beautifully fresh beer battered flathead and one of Tassie's finest pinots: Kelly's!

'On most footy nights,
an unusual tension exists'

BEER BATTERED FLATTIE

This is a wonderful summer specialty. It is great served with a green salad and some mayonnaise, or even a dollop of the yoghurt sauce on page 26. Washed down with a few cold beers while watching the cricket, of course.

BATTER
1 ³/₄ cups (265 g) self raising flour
1 cup (250 ml) beer

1 cup (250 ml) water
vegetable oil, to deep fry
4 flathead fillets (about 150 g each)

To make the batter, sift the flour into a bowl, and make a well in the centre. Gradually add the beer and water, whisking to combine. Set aside for a few minutes.

Half fill a large saucepan with vegetable oil, and heat over medium high temperature. Using one pair of tongs, dip a fillet into the batter, let the excess drip off briefly, then put into the oil. Cook for 4-5 minutes, depending on the thickness of the fillet, until golden brown. Lift from the oil with another pair of tongs or a slotted spoon, and drain on paper towels. You should be able to cook two at once, but don't overcrowd the pan.

Note: You can vary this recipe by replacing some of the flour (about ¹/₄ cup) with chickpea flour, and adding a good pinch of your favourite curry powder.

SERVES 4

THE
SNAPPER
KING

Kell and I first met Andrew Mirosch when we were developing a love for Stradbroke Island and he was a chef there at the Whale's Way Restaurant. It was there that we began our friendship and, later, we became really good fishing mates. For the record, although he is a much better cook than I am, there is absolutely no question that I am the Snapper King.

Andrew is a now a columnist, a TV presenter and the chef at the Sirromet multi-award-winning restaurant Lurleen's, which is nestled in the hills of picturesque Mount Cotton, a fine region between Brisbane and the Gold Coast. Lurleen's has recently won two Awards of Excellence and has been named as Queensland's Best Restaurant in a Winery and Queensland's Best Tourism Restaurant. Those awards speak for themselves.

Because of our busy lifestyles, we don't often get the chance to go fishing any more, but there has been a lot of jousting about it in the media. Hopefully, I'll have the last laugh in this little segment of the book!

Andrew's great strength in cooking is that he lets the produce shine without really hammering the flavours of the food by over-spicing. He has a good balance in his food, which is something I've learnt from him. Sometimes, less is better. If you have great-quality produce, you're very lucky – and fortune certainly smiles on Lurleen's. Much of the produce is grown there and the chefs have access to beautiful fresh fruit and vegetables. Nearby, the Redlands area, too, grows wonderful produce, like the mouth-watering strawberries and fantastic, fresh green vegetables. Andrew uses these in his cooking.

What better chef could I have chosen to prepare a surprise family celebration for Mum and Dad's fortieth wedding anniversary?

'Although Andrew is a much better cook than I am, there is absolutely no question that I am the Snapper King!'

UDON PRAWN SALAD

This is such a simple and refreshingly 'zingy' salad to have on a hot summer day.

500 g fresh udon noodles

1 tablespoon sesame seeds

1 tablespoon olive oil

1/2 teaspoon sesame oil

1/2 cup coriander leaves, roughly chopped

1 small red onion, finely sliced

2 spring onions, finely sliced

500 g cooked prawns, peeled

1 tablespoon lime juice

2 red bird's-eye chillies, seeded and finely chopped

lime wedges, to serve

Prepare the noodles as directed on the packet. Toast the sesame seeds in a dry frying pan over medium heat for about 2 minutes, until golden brown. Transfer to a plate to cool.

Drain the noodles and place into a large bowl. Add the olive oil and sesame oil and toss to coat. Add the remaining ingredients and toss to combine. Serve with the lime quarters.

SERVES 2-3

NOTE

You can buy udon noodles from the supermarket, either in the fridge section, or on the shelf with other Asian ingredients, vacuum packed. Preparation instructions vary, but as they are pre-cooked they usually only need to be rinsed under hot water to separate the strands.

THE PIZZA GUY

I was sure the Kiwis finally had a plan. With one game remaining in the one-day series, we were leading 4-0 and the enthusiasts from the Land of the Long White Cloud were hoping someone, anyone, would come up with an idea to put the Aussies off their game and restore some Kiwi pride.

'The boys wanted The Pizza Guy's scalp, or a few pizzas slung their way'

All was revealed the moment our 'luxurious limos' (aka the catering vans) entered the stadium. Parking outside behind the changing rooms, ready and waiting to do battle with the Aussies, was New Zealand's last hope: The Pizza Guy.

The Aussie team began telling each other pizza stories. I recalled, lightheartedly, how after a heavy loss to Queensland, Victoria's dietician had asked each of the players in the losers' dressing room what he had eaten the night before.

Dean Jones had replied: 'Just a small plate of spaghetti and, er … some of those other healthy options that were provided.'

Next, Merv Hughes faced the human lie detector. 'Now, Merv, what about you?' asked the dietician. 'Me?' answered Merv in a quietly muffled tone as if butter wouldn't melt in his mouth. 'I only had a family pizza.'

'Yes,' nodded the dietician, who had picked up on the 'pizza' but not on the 'family'. 'And how many pieces of that did you have, Merv?'

'Well, that depends,' said Merv as he pulled off his smelly socks and leaned back, fully relaxed.

'What do you mean, depends?' replied his inquisitor.

'Depends on how many pieces they cut it into!'

After that story, our thoughts returned to The Pizza Guy as one Aussie player after another said: 'That's it!' 'The Kiwis are attacking our stomachs!' 'Of all the low acts.' 'Only a Kiwi!'

First, The Pizza Guy deployed smoke-screen tactics as he cranked up New Zealand's first mobile wood-fired pizza service. The Kiwis had done their homework well, as usual, attacking our lungs, a massive area of concern for me personally as I had only just got my nose across the line to tour after being struck down with pneumonia and pleurisy. The second wave of attack came soon after, as swift and precise as the first. The aroma of freshly baked pizza wafted in and around the changing room – an unbearable, tantalising, distracting scent!

Now, the Australian cricket team strongly believes that the best form of defence is attack. It just so happened that I was a non-player that day, ruled out with extensive oedema around the soft tissues surrounding the acromioclavicular joint and distal third of the clavicle, predominantly within the subcutaneous fat, extending laterally and distally over the outer margin of the deltoid muscle. In other words, I was laid low with a bloody sore shoulder. I was pretty much useless for anything apart from finding out about our latest opponent. The boys wanted The Pizza Guy's scalp or, at the very least, a few pizzas slung their way. In no position to argue, I ventured into enemy territory.

The Pizza Guy was certainly running a well-oiled unit: a state-of-the-art mobile pizza oven that had been imported from Germany. He was punching out a pizza every 30 seconds. I knew a deal had to be made swiftly so I confidently ambled up to him and started talking, sprinkling a few good Aussie words here and there to help him identify me.

'Mate, if you let me cook half a dozen pizzas, I'll supply the toppings. I'll even let you come into the Aussie change rooms for a few beers and take a few snaps showcasing your business. What do you reckon? Fair enough?'

'Done,' he replied.

How easy was that? Now he was working for us. A win-win situation. To quote from Sun Tzu, the ancient Chinese philosopher of war who regularly pops up in coach John Buchanan's pre-game team-meeting notes, the definition of true excellence is 'to plan secretly, to move surreptitiously, to foil the enemy's intentions and baulk his schemes so that, at last, the day may be won without shedding a drop of blood'.

The Pizza Guy had been given a better offer and, as per the promise, I made the pizzas and delivered them fresh to our change room, a stone's throw away, to be enjoyed after a record-breaking 5-0 series win to Australia. As any full-blooded Aussie would say: 'You bloody beauty!'

PRAWN PITA PIZZA

4 large pita breads
1 cup (250 g) crème fraiche
1/2 cup (90 g) sundried tomatoes, drained
lime juice, to taste

salt and pepper
500 g peeled banana (or medium) prawns
1 red onion, finely sliced
capers, optional
extra virgin olive oil
salt and cracked black pepper
torn basil leaves

Preheat the oven to 220C. If you have a pizza stone, place it in the oven to preheat. Combine the crème fraiche and sundried tomatoes in a food processor, season with a squeeze of lime juice and salt and pepper to taste. Process until smooth.

Lightly flour the underneath of the pita breads. Spread the sundried tomato paste onto the pita breads, and top with prawns and onion. Place into the oven (on pizza trays if you don't have a stone), and bake for 10 minutes, until the prawns are cooked through and the bread is golden brown and crisp.

To serve, scatter capers over, if using, and drizzle with olive oil. Season to taste and top with basil leaves. Serve immediately.

SERVES 4

BIRTHDAY GIRL

When you and your wife have been together for a long time and her birthday comes along, what do you do? Push the panic button and go into stress mode? I reckon just about every bloke out there can relate to that. Men will surely understand the feeling that it's virtually impossible to buy a suitable present. Everything you think of, she already has! Desperation creeps in. And then despair. You feel that you are wasting your time in some ways, because you've got absolutely no idea what to do. Well, I have the answer!

It was Kell's thirtieth birthday and she was in the last two weeks of her pregnancy with Josh. I thought of going out somewhere … anywhere! But that was a little bit daunting: what if the baby decided to make an appearance earlier than anticipated! A trip away was out of the question for the same reason, so I

put my thinking cap on. 'Eureka!' I thought. 'Rather than Mohammad going to the mountain, the mountain can come to Mohammad!'

My plan was simple but perfect: I organised for caterers from the James Street Cooking School to come to our home and prepare a private dinner for two! How great was that? The solution to every male's birthday problems.

It was a fantastic experience because we were in the comfort of our own home and the food was superb. The chef cooked the most incredible scallop dish and also a steak dish. And, of course, we had access to our very own cellar. It was wonderful. Even though we eat out often, it was one of our top nights of all time. First class.

What better birthday present? And a really special night.

juice of 1 lime

1 tablespoon olive oil

1 red chilli, finely chopped

1 garlic clove, finely chopped

$\frac{1}{2}$ teaspoon grated fresh ginger

1 teaspoon ground cumin

pinch each of sugar, salt and freshly ground
black pepper

1 cup (200 g) long grain white rice (jasmine
is good)

300 ml coconut milk, approximately

36 scallops

12 cleaned double scallop shells

extra lime juice, to serve

coriander leaves, to garnish

Preheat a BBQ plate. Combine the lime juice, olive oil, chilli, garlic, ginger, cumin and seasonings in a small food processor or mortar and pestle and blend until smooth.

To make the coconut rice, place the rice and 1 cup (250 ml) of the coconut milk into a large saucepan. Add 1 cup (250 ml) of cold water (or fish or vegie stock if you like), cover and bring to the boil. Reduce the heat to low and cook for 6 minutes, then turn off the heat and stand, covered, for 10 minutes.

Place three scallops into each shell. Place a teaspoon of the spice mixture onto the scallops, along with a teaspoon of coconut milk. Put the shells onto the BBQ plate. Once the liquid starts to bubble inside the shells, time them to cook for about 30 seconds. The scallops will be white when cooked, but take care not to overcook them.

Serve with the coconut rice, an extra squeeze of lime juice and garnish with coriander.

SERVES 4

NICKNAMES AND FAVOURITE FOODS

Nicknames and food are specialities of the Aussie cricket team, so I thought I'd take time to tell you a bit about them. My nickname is very simple – Haydos, which gets shortened to Dos. Jurassic, too, is another favourite (because they reckon I've got a big body and little head, much like a dinosaur!). My favourite meal is Kell's chicken casserole (if you want the recipe, it's in my first book!).

RICKY PONTING: Punter, because he bets on horses, dogs, fleas … anything! Punter loves his roast pork.

ADAM GILCHRIST: Gilly, and also Churchie. He gets called Churchie because during the '97 Ashes Series, Steve Waugh, Matthew Elliot and Adam, on completion of a tour game against Gloucestershire at Bristol Oval, bumped into a group of kids who, with great delight and eyes wide open, said to Steve, 'Ee, you're that Steve Waugh.' Then they turned to Matthew: 'You're that Matthew Elliot.' Next was Gilly, and the little blokes exclaimed, 'Ee, you're that Eric Gillchurch!' Gilly's favourite meal would be a toss up between penne arrabbiata or Mel's stir fry Thai curry with the full monty of poppadums and condiments.

JUSTIN LANGER: Alfie, after Alfie Langer, the rugby league legend. We also call him Midge, as in midget, because he is so small. The Barmy Army are going to be all over him again in summer with their hilarious taunting songs. My two favourites are 'Hi-Ho! Hi-Ho! It's Off to Work We Go' (from Disney's *Snow White and the Seven Dwarfs*) and 'You're So Small It's Unbelievable!'. The boys reckon that Alfie is such a 'brown nose' that he'd say his favourite food is anything that I cook. (Harsh, Alf. Harsh! I know its Sue's seafood.)

GLENN MCGRATH: Because we reckon his legs look like a pigeon's, naturally we call him Pidge. He also gets called Mr Squiggle (after the old ABC TV children's character) since he's long and skinny like a pencil and, in answer to his beloved wife's requests he promptly replies, 'Yes, Miss Jane?'. Pidge's partial to anything that's been seared on a barbie.

DAMIEN MARTYN: Marto, for obvious reasons. His meal of choice would be steak and mushrooms: I have never known anyone who loves mushrooms as much as Marto!

SHANE WATSON: Watto, and Prince Charming out of the movie *Shrek 2*, because he's the spitting image of him. Watto will eat anything – he'd be hard pushed to pick a favourite dish!

SIMON KATICH: Katto, and Stiffy, because of his prolonged problems with a 'frozen' neck. Although Katto was born without the sense of smell, surprisingly he's retained his sense of taste and, like Watto, is such a good 'doer' on the food stakes.

When I asked him about his favourite food, he replied, 'Mate, you'd have to go through the top ten not just one!' He finally narrowed it down to his old man's lamb on a spit with roast potatoes and steamed fresh green beans with loads of salt.

ANDREW SYMONDS: Simmo, and Roy, after the basketball star Leroy Loggins. He loves tucking into a t-bone with mashed potatoes and plain gravy, and for dessert he reckons his mum's lemon meringue pie is a bit of alright!

SHANE WARNE: Warney, SK, and The King. Margherita pizza would have to be his favourite when overseas, as he doesn't trust anyone on 'enemy' territory! On home soil he prefers to savour a Hawaiian pizza topped with very finely shredded ham, or hot chips on a bread roll with loads of butter and tomato sauce.

BRAD HOGG: Hoggy, and George. George is actually Hoggy's first name, but he can't stand it so goes by his middle name instead. He's a good country boy so meat and three veg is good to go for Hoggy – the plainer the better.

JASON GILLESPIE: Dizzy, after Dizzy Gillespie, the jazz master. However, we reckon our Dizzy is completely tone deaf, hence his love of all heavy metal rock bands! We've banned him from choosing the vibe music for the dressing room! Jason will tuck into bangers and mash with gusto every time.

BRAD HODGE: Dodgem, because of his love affair with the used car industry. Brad just loves spaghetti marinara.

MICHAEL CLARKE: Young Pup, and Milky because of his porcelain complexion. (Sorry, Pup!) He rates his Mum's beef rissoles, mashed potatoes, veg and gravy as his all-time favourite meal, though tacos come a close second. One thing's for sure, Pup is always on the lookout for 'wingmen' to dine out at Mexican restaurants when we're on tour.

MICHAEL HUSSEY: Mr Cricket, because he is a complete and utter cricket tragic. Simmo reckons his favourite meal would be cricket ball sandwiches, but Mr Cricket claims it's spaghetti marinara!

BRETT LEE: Binga, after the retail chain Bing Lee. He votes wife Liz's shepherd's pie as his top dish, because it's cooked with love. Ah, newlyweds. It's lovely!

STUART MACGILL: Grape Juice, after his affection for a good bottle of vino. We also call him Robocop, because of his running style. He's rather fond of grass-fed Riverina beef fillet with truffled mash!

MICHAEL KASPROWICZ: Kaspa, Slobadam Smellavinavich, and Salami Boy. There are a few more too: Back Tank, Sub Tank, Fuel Tank, Bottom, after his well-rounded chaise. Kaspa loves a good antipasto platter, and just about anything that takes a long time to eat and enjoy, like a leisurely morning breakfast with great coffee and all the daily newspapers.

250 g dried rice noodles

¹/₄ cup (60 ml) fish sauce

¹/₄ cup (60 ml) sweet chilli sauce

2 teaspoons peanut butter

3 tablespoons safflower oil

1 tablespoon tamarind sauce (optional)

3 garlic cloves, crushed

1-2 red chillies, seeded and finely chopped

1 chicken breast fillet, finely sliced

10-12 green prawns, peeled, tails left intact

2 eggs, lightly beaten

2 spring onions, finely sliced

100 g bean sprouts

¹/₂ cup coriander, chopped

¹/₂ cup (80 g) chopped peanuts

lime wedges, to serve

extra sweet chilli sauce, to serve

Place the noodles into a large heatproof bowl, cover with boiling water and soak for 10 minutes. Combine the fish sauce, sweet chilli sauce and peanut butter; set aside.

Heat the oil in a large wok, and add the tamarind sauce if using. Stir fry the garlic, chillies, chicken and prawns over high heat for about 3 minutes, until cooked through. Add the eggs and stir fry until just set and kind of scrambled.

Add the noodles and sauce mixture to the wok, and stir fry for 1 minute, until well combined. Toss through most of the spring onions, bean sprouts, coriander and peanuts, reserving some for garnish.

Serve topped with the reserved ingredients, with lime wedges and extra sweet chilli sauce on the side.

SERVES 2-3

THE BAXTER RECIPE FOR SUCCESS

Picture this: It was a gloomy, overcast day in Edinburgh, Scotland — and the dark clouds were not only outside. We had just drawn the third Test but the Poms were all over us like festering chickenpox and gaining momentum in the Ashes series. The weather bureau was forecasting continuing rain, and we had a one-day international against Scotland scheduled. Whatever the weather, this was to be my game off and my good friend Allan Lamb had invited me to go salmon fishing with him and his son, Richie, at Gordon Baxter's private 'beat'. The Baxters of Speyside have three royal warrants to their name and create wonderful soups, jams and preserves for which they have become world famous. They also lease a magnificent portion of the River Spey, home of some of the best salmon fishing in Scotland. But I had no way of getting there, so I was stuck in my hotel room, sad, sorry and disappointed.

Then the phone rang. It was Gordon Baxter, president of the company. Having heard of my dilemma, he had organised transport for me to the Scottish

Highlands. I soon found myself travelling through one of the most beautiful places in the country courtesy of a generous and hospitable businessman whom I had not yet met. Those gloomy clouds started lifting.

The tiny Morayshire village of Fochabers is a picturesque place, with the majestic river rushing down from the misty Grampian Mountains, running through cattle-grazing land on its race of 172 kilometres to the Moray Firth at Spey Bay.

At my destination — the splendid Lord March Pool on the Baxters' bonny part of the river, with the unusual red sandstone cliffs in the background — there was another sight to behold: Lamby! He looked absolutely resplendent, like a 'good sort', in the traditional, full-tartan Scottish outfit, complete with all the trimmings. He could see by the smirk on my face that I was ready to rip into him with a good old Aussie dig.

'Just look at you, you big …! You've changed; I know you have!'

'Naaah!' he laughed, as only Lamby could. 'Ya big wallaby!'

I first met Lamby when I captained Northamptonshire and he is very much a part of that extended cricketing family I spoke about in my last book. I knew his invitation was not just about catching salmon. He was also trying to support me at a time when I was struggling for form. Of course his loyalty is to England but, like a true friend, he was there for me. I can still hear his encouraging South African-cum-English-accented words. There was even an Aussie flavour thrown in. He spoke optimistically about the future and the runs I was going to score. 'Maa-aate!' he drawled, Aussie style. 'Relax! It's gonna happen!'

And then the competition was on. When I'm fishing with Lamby, I can't resist trying to get one up on him and this was definitely my day. Did I give him grief! The excuses rushed out of his mouth almost as fast as the River Spey raced by. 'Can't see!', 'It's raining!', 'Too slow!', 'Too low!'

At last it happened. A bite. I had actually thought Lamby was taking me down and I had not been impressed but I need not have worried. There is a traditional ceremony associated with catching your first Spey fish. They call the first one the 'virgin' fish and the fisherman is said to have 'lost his virginity'! The virgin fish is killed and blooded. Then the dead fish and the blood are smeared over the catcher's face. It's all part of the experience and I joined in the laughter and fun. Much to Lamby's disgust, I went on to hook a second fish. More ribbing for poor old Lamby. He didn't catch a single fish that day.

The dismal cloud that had been hanging over me that morning turned out to have a silver lining: I met a great man that day. I will remember Gordon Baxter for the rest of my life, and not only because he shares my love for cricket and good, wholesome food. He gave me a special day in my friendship with Lamby as well as the amazing experience of fishing for salmon on the River Spey. And there is more. At a sumptuous buffet lunch, he allowed me to savour some of his delicious, homemade Scottish culinary delights, and he has given me permission to share with you a Baxters recipe for salmon quiche.

Maybe we can all learn something, too, from Gordon Baxter's recipe for business success: 'Try to be the best. That's the only place to be: the top of the heap.'

And you know, just as Lamby had predicted, I did go on to make more runs — runs that, perhaps, saved my career.

BAXTERS SALMON QUICHE

PASTRY

170 g plain flour

110 g butter

pinch of salt

1 egg yolk

1 tablespoon iced water

FILLING

50 g butter

1 small onion, diced

1 small leek, diced

1 tablespoon fresh thyme leaves

1 tablespoon chopped chives

3 eggs

$1/2$ cup (125 ml) cream

250 g piece hot smoked salmon

$1/2$ cup (50 g) finely grated Parmesan cheese

To make the pastry, rub the flour, butter and salt together until it resembles fine breadcrumbs. Add the combined egg yolk and water and cut through with a knife until evenly moistened. Gather the dough together to gently shape into a round disc. Wrap in plastic and refrigerate for 1 hour.

Preheat the oven to 180C. Roll out the dough to fit a 23 cm round loose bottom flan tin. Line with a sheet of non-stick baking paper, and fill with dried rice or beans. Bake for 10 minutes, then remove the paper and beans and bake a further 10 minutes. Reduce the oven to 160C.

To make the filling, melt the butter in a frying pan and cook the onion, leek, thyme and chives until soft. Flake the salmon into the pan, then spread into the pastry case. Stand the tin on a flat baking tray.

Beat the eggs and cream together and pour over the salmon mixture. Bake for 30 minutes until set and lightly golden, then sprinkle with the cheese and cook a further 5 minutes.

SERVES 6-8

IN FRONT OF THE CAMERA

We arrived home from England with a few days to spare before the start of the Super Series and then the filming started for the Ford 'backyard cricket' ads.

Now, most people don't know that these were actually filmed in our backyard. With the help of a few props, skilful set designers can do magical things and, as a result, the final product didn't look anything like our backyard.

It's unbelievable how much effort goes into one 15-second commercial. Two days of working three to four hours a day! It baffles me when I look at a movie now. How much time would it take to produce? How many trucks, cars, cameras, catering vans? They were all there at our place. They even started arriving the day before! Grace was in her element and Kell and I had heaps of fun, too.

Lights, camera, action! Enter Michael Clarke (Pup) and me. Both of us like to entertain but the amazing part was that we were just being ourselves, no acting required! Pup was cheeky in the commercial and that's exactly what he is like. I was competitive and that's me! The funniest part was when I said, 'Aw, Mum …', which was like resurrecting a scene from the past, arguing over a backyard decision and calling on Mum to be the umpire. It brought back memories of my brother Gary and me playing backyard cricket together as boys.

It never ceases to amaze me just how much interest there is in these commercials. They always pop up in the middle of Test matches, during the drinks breaks. Now, that's when I really am under the pump. The boys, just waiting to have a bit of fun, mill around. 'Hey! Here's Haydos! What are you doing on the screen, Haydos? This'll be good!'

But I can handle them. After all, 'All the world's a stage, and all the men and women merely players …'

'Pup was cheeky in the commercial, and that is exactly what he is like. I was competitive, and that's me!'

KERRY

PACKER

He has been called a smart entrepreneur, a risk-taker, a national larrikin, a confrontational businessman, a compulsive gambler, a spontaneous philanthropist, the most successful businessman of our generation. In the 1970s, he not only created World Series Cricket but also changed the game's image forever. He revolutionised television coverage of cricket (indeed, of sport in general) and even the way the game was played.

So when Alan Jones, a friend of Kerry Packer's, dined with Kell and me at our home, the dinner conversation soon turned to the one-day game and the inspirational figure behind World Series Cricket.

'Mate, I'd absolutely love to meet Kerry Packer,' I said.

Next thing I know, Alan has organised for me to meet the great man. I was absolutely honoured. I invited my old friends Steve Waugh (Tugger) and Justin Langer (Alfie) and a couple of the younger fellas, Brett Lee (Binga) and Shane Watson (Watto), to join me.

Now, the Aussie team is divided into Nerds (traditional, conservative dressers) and Julios (slick, modern ones). Dressing sharp, streaking hair and using gel is left to the Julios, and for the rest of us Nerds, what to wear isn't usually part of the conversation. When we asked what we should wear for this occasion, we were told 'something casual and comfortable'. Binga and Watto, members of the young brigade and fully fledged Julios, did exactly that. Tugger (ex-Nerd) wore a suit and tie and, despite what was said, Alfie and I wore our Aussie suits and ties.

'Nerds'— and proud of the name! We were meeting a legend. This was an event. This was the most interesting bloke in cricket; the man who had changed what our cricketing lives are all about today. Out of absolute respect for him, we dressed for the occasion.

As you can see, we were certainly not taking this affair lightly and as we waited to meet Kerry, the atmosphere was electric. We also felt a little nervous, not because it was the night before the Super Series Test but because we were meeting a very skilled tactician. After all, we'd heard a few stories! Kerry Packer would have an opportunity to put us all in the hot seat, especially on the subject of cricket!

Once we'd arrived at his home and had all been introduced to the great man, Alan and Kerry engaged in some enjoyable verbal jousting. Then Kerry turned to Tugger, who'd just finished writing his autobiography, and said 'Son, who's opening your book launch?'

'The Prime Minister, Mr Packer.'.

Kerry looked over at Alan and said, 'Well, Mr President, that's put you in your place!'

Before long, the conversation turned to cricket. Alfie was on the mat. 'Son,' said Kerry, 'explain to me why you get hit on the helmet so much.'

Poor old Alfie! He was quietly taken aback and mumbled 'I … er … don't … really know.'

'Son,' responded Kerry, intent on getting straight to the point. 'You just can't be watching the ball.'

We looked apprehensively at each other. Tugger smirked. One down: three to go!

Kerry's belief in good luck, nurtured by his incredible gambling feats, was known to all of us, and it featured in the conversation. We were talking about Tony Greig's development of helmets. It was a significant part of the discourse and Kerry would not let it go. Just when Alfie thought he could relax, Kerry, with a twinkle in his eye, turned to him again. 'And, son, you should know all about luck. If Greig hadn't invented helmets, you'd be ******* dead!'

The rest of us were left unscathed. We had all dined out on Alfie!

The whole experience was a cracker. That one short meeting left a lasting impression on me. Kerry Packer was a great Australian who flew the Aussie flag high. He was a straight-shooter, an incredibly knowledgeable man and a wonderful communicator. He had a passion for the subjects about which he spoke, and you couldn't help but be drawn in. His opinions were strong and confronting. We were like a bunch of naughty schoolboys wondering just who was going to get it! But we were proud of our achievements and Kerry was a great example of what could be done through hard work, determination and sheer Aussie grit.

Sadly, he died on Boxing Day in 2005. As the Australian team donned black armbands for the second day of the Test against South Africa, to pay tribute to Kerry Packer, I could hear the words of that World Series Cricket theme song, 'Come On, Aussie, Come On', and with a great sense of pride, mixed with humility, I could hear Kerry's last words to me: 'Son, thank you so much for taking the time to come and meet me.' I knew in my heart that I would go on to make a century in that match.

Kerry Packer was a true blue, fair dinkum Aussie icon – a man among men.

'Son, explain to me why you get hit on the helmet so much'

58

KP MEAT PIE

Serve this with peas and
carrots, and don't be
afraid to sprinkle on a little
Worcestershire sauce or chilli
sauce, to your taste.

$^1/_3$ cup (50 g) plain flour
salt and freshly ground black pepper
500 g blade or chuck steak, cut into 3 cm cubes
2 tablespoons olive oil
3 bacon rashers, chopped
2 onions, chopped

3 garlic cloves, finely chopped
2 cups (500 ml) beef or vegetable stock
2 sprigs rosemary
$^1/_2$ cup (125 ml) red wine
4 sheets frozen puff pastry, thawed

Put the flour into a plastic bag, season the flour with salt and pepper and add the meat. Twist the opening to seal, and shake to coat. Take the pieces out and shake off the excess. Heat half the oil in a large pan and cook the meat in 2 batches over moderately high heat until brown. Set aside.

Add the remaining oil, and cook the bacon until browned; set aside. Cook the onions and garlic over medium heat until soft and lightly browned. Return the steak and bacon to the pan, then add the stock gradually, stirring and scraping the bottom of the pan.

Add the rosemary and wine, cover and bring just to the boil. Turn the heat down to low and simmer for 1 $^1/_2$ hours. Uncover and cook a further 30 minutes, until the meat is very tender. Cool completely before assembling the pie. This mixture could be made a day in advance, and the pie made the next day (it tastes better that way as well).

Preheat the oven to 200C. Line a 23 cm, 4 cup capacity pie dish with a sheet of pastry. It won't cover the dish completely so make sure 2 sides are covered, then cut 2 wide strips from another sheet to cover the rest. Make sure you overlap the pastry well and press the joins together. Fill with the meat mixture.

Cut the remaining pastry into strips, and use to top the pie in a lattice pattern. The easiest way to do this is to lay out the strips on a sheet of baking paper, weaving them together. You'll need to join the strips so that they are long enough to cover the pie dish. When it is done, use the paper to help flip it onto the pie. Press the edges and trim away the excess pastry. If this all seems too much, you can just top with a sheet of pastry, but make sure you cut some slits in the top to allow steam to escape.

Bake for 10 minutes, then reduce the heat to 180C and cook a further 50-60 minutes, until golden brown.

SERVES 6

FIELD OF DREAMS

Growing up, we all have our dreams. As a little fella, I only ever wanted two things: to be a farmer like my dad and to play cricket for Australia. I have amazing memories of long days on the farm with Dad, sitting up beside him, helping him with the peanuts and eating lots of them, too. I can still recall the two of us coming home one day after having just had the best afternoon, playing the likes of Charlie Pride (even Kamal got a gig!) in the air-conditioned tractor, listening to his stories, and stopping every now and then to fork-in the ends of peanut rows. That day, I raced inside, covered from head to toe in red soil. Mum said later all she could see were my blue eyes. 'How good was that, Mum? I can hardly wait to be 16, leave school and become a farmer!' I was happy and thought I had my whole future 'signed, sealed and delivered'. (Mum and Dad later confessed they had not wanted me to develop a love for farming. They really wanted me to get a good education and have all the kinds of opportunities that brings.)

In time, I realised my two dreams couldn't go together. After all, there are no Test matches played in Kingaroy. But I loved my childhood home. It was fun, especially growing up with my big brother, Gary. We had all kinds of adventures.

I enjoyed my home town as well, and I still like the drive home, approximately three hours from Brisbane. My dad has cattle on his property now but, as I've said, when I was a little critter, we had peanuts. Kingaroy has the best peanuts in the world. I reckon I've tried peanuts from every country and I'm a fair judge! Thinking about it now, though, Dad should have started in the cattle industry sooner, with two hungry boys to feed. Whenever we drive home to Kingaroy, I always find myself saying to Kell: 'It makes me hungry just looking at those cows!' I've always loved beautiful fresh meat. There is nothing better than a barbeque and a cold beer on a hot summer's day.

Who knows where our dreams can take us? I'm sure at this stage, our daughter, Grace, who is four, thinks she is going to be a ballerina for half her life and a skateboard rider for the other half. Of course, I'm hoping that turns into surfboard riding and I can travel the world with her. (Only kidding, Kell!)

As for our son, Joshua, at just over a year old, I think his goal is to eat his way into the record books. My mum and dad say I came into the world with a knife and fork in my hands, so perhaps it's in the genes! He's such a great little doer, too — a real little champ!

And Kell? She just wants the best for all of us.

But there's one thing I'm sure of — with love, support, commitment, really hard work and strong determination, it is possible 'to dream the impossible dream' and to 'reach the impossible star'. I know. I've done it!

'As a little fella, I only ever wanted two things: to be a farmer like my dad, and to play cricket for Australia'

PORK SALAD WITH SALT AND VINEGAR PEANUTS

If you can't find salt and vinegar peanuts, there are other flavours you can get, such as balsamic vinegar, or chilli. You can even use plain nuts if you like.

MARINADE

1 tablespoon finely chopped ginger

4 garlic cloves, finely chopped

1 red chilli, finely chopped

1 tablespoon olive oil

1/2 teaspoon salt

1/2 teaspoon pepper

2 small pork fillets (about 200 g each)

1 cup (100 g) shredded red cabbage

1/2 iceberg lettuce, shredded

1 cup (75 g) bean sprouts

1/2 bunch coriander leaves, chopped

1/2 red onion, finely sliced

1 tablespoon olive oil, extra

1 tablespoon lime juice

1 cup (160 g) finely chopped salt and vinegar peanuts

Combine the marinade ingredients in a non-metallic dish and add the pork fillets. Cover and marinate for about 30 minutes. Cook on a hot BBQ, chargrill or frying pan for 10 minutes. Set aside to rest.

Place the cabbage, lettuce, bean sprouts, coriander and onion in a large bowl and toss to combine. Arrange onto serving plates or a platter. Thinly slice the pork and place on top of the salad. Drizzle with olive oil and lime juice, and sprinkle with the nuts. Serve immediately.

SERVES 4

THE GREATEST SLEDGE

I was playing at the SCG in one of the dead-rubber games of the 2005 VB one-day series. We had won the toss and batted first and I was opening with Gilly. I reckon I scored about 40 off 55 balls, which is fair going for an opening batsman, but I could see why the crowd was getting agitated. Gilly, at the other end, was red hot and it would have been like watching the highlights from one end only. 'Chalk and cheese' come to mind. I was batting solidly but not setting the world on fire. At the time, my position in the team was coming under question and the spectators were definitely on my case, to the point where I got booed off the ground by my home Aussie crowd.

Change of innings: the opposition got through the first 15 overs and I was out on the square-leg boundary, getting heckled big-time by this one bloke who was sitting high up in the Dougie Walters stand. He yelled, ''Ey, 'ayden! Yer batting's ****!'

Well, everyone is entitled to his own opinion, I thought.

But he wasn't letting up. ''Ey, 'ayden! Can ya 'ear me?'

I could hear him all right. Everyone in the SCG could!

'Ya should be outta the team. Give someone else a go! Give Katich a go, yer dill!' he bawled, as he downed another beer. I was totally ignoring him, giving him absolutely nothing, until finally he bellowed like a bull: 'And, 'ayden, by the way, yer chicken casserole tastes like ****!'

That was it! I just had to laugh. His persistence had paid off. I couldn't resist a reply and turned around, shouting back: 'Well, you bought it, you mug!' I added as politely as I could under the circumstances: 'Oh, and by the way, thanks for the 30 bucks. I'll have a beer on you tonight, you clown!'

The crowd loved it. So did I!

'I was getting heckled big time by this one bloke high up in the Dougie Walters stand'

VEAL STEW WITH PARSLEY DUMPLINGS

I like to use an enamelled, cast iron casserole dish, which will
go from the stove top to the oven (less washing up!). If you
don't have one, you can cook on the stove in a large saucepan,
then transfer the mixture to an ordinary casserole dish for the
oven part.

½ cup (75 g) plain flour
salt and freshly ground black pepper
1 kg veal casserole steak, cut into 3cm cubes
¼ cup (60 ml) olive oil
2 onions, chopped
1 large carrot, chopped
2 stalks celery, chopped
4 garlic cloves, finely chopped
4 cups (1L) vegetable or veal stock

1 cup (250 ml) red wine
2 sprigs rosemary

DUMPLINGS

2 cups (300 g) self raising flour
40 g butter
1 cup parsley, chopped
salt and freshly ground black pepper
¾ cup (185 ml) water

Preheat the oven to 150C. Season the flour with salt and pepper. Roll the meat in the flour to coat,
and shake off the excess. Heat 1 tablespoon of the oil in a large (12 cup capacity) flameproof casserole
dish. Cook the meat in 4 batches over moderately high heat until brown, adding more oil as necessary.
Set aside.

Cook the onion, celery, carrot and garlic over medium heat for about 10 minutes, until they start to
soften and become lightly golden. Return the meat to the pan along with the stock and wine, stirring
and scraping the bottom of the pan. Bring just to the boil, then place in the oven and cook, covered,
for 3 hours, until the meat is very tender. Increase the oven heat to 200C.

To make the dumplings, put the flour into a large bowl and rub in the butter. Stir in the parsley and salt
and pepper. Add enough of the water to make a soft, slightly sticky dough. Carefully drop spoonfuls of
the dough into the casserole. Cook uncovered for 20 minutes, until risen and lightly golden.

SERVES 6

ANYTHING TO PASS THE TIME

'Kaspa always comes up with something inventive, and he had an idea that was a beauty'

Another Test, another toss! Excitement all around — we're fired up and ready to confront the opposition. The umpires walk out, stoically. It's time! With a touch of our Aussie flag, a few warm-ups and a quick prayer, Alfie and I walk proudly to centre pitch. Alfie takes strike. A quick single. I prepare my wicket, do the usual housekeeping, take time to look around and, when I'm good and ready and have the opening bowler seething, I take strike. Another single. What was that I felt? Oh no … rain! Back to the pavilion. It's pouring, coming down in buckets. The covers come out and we're cooked (jargon in keeping with theme of book!) till late in the afternoon. I knew you'd ask how we pass the time …

Now, Michael Kasprowicz, Kaspa for short, my good Aussie teammate (even though he is a bowler) with fine Queensland blood flowing through his veins, always comes up with something inventive and, while we were waiting to play in Mumbai, he had an idea that was a beauty. It even went international — to England, right through the Ashes series. It was called the Mumbai Mumbler and Kaspa became the in-house snitch journalist and editor-in-chief. Ruthless rumours, gossip and indeed anything at all untoward were collected methodically, filed meticulously, written ridiculously, edited unethically and flaunted flawlessly for all to read in the publication's change-room circulation.

Another time-passer: at the start of the World Cup Series tour, we all contributed to buying a good-quality team stereo to play our favourite music. Now, there was a slight problem: someone always had to carry the stereo onto the plane as it couldn't be packed in our luggage. It became quite a pain in the butt! We devised all kinds of games to sort out who would get the job. And so we had the scissors-paper-rock tournament – this was an elimination series so if you lost a round, you went back into the pool and if you won, you sat down. Finally, there would be one person who had to carry the stereo. If you didn't take the game seriously – chucking a third finger in, for example – that meant an automatic re-entry to the pool. You could take the rap to get a laugh, but you still remained in the running.

'Mozzie' Marbo (Jimmy Maher), another fine Queenslander, came up with one of the best games I've ever seen during the World Cup. Marbo has a great sense of humour and calls a horse race well. First, he devised names for each 'horse', or Aussie cricket team member, and he gave each runner a barrier. Then he organised a sweep. He went on to call the race, picking on the worst, funniest or silliest characteristics of each of us. 'And they're off! First out is the big-eared, old working mare from Perth [Gilly] …' He had us in stitches. Anything to pass the time!

RISSOLES

These are easy to make and very versatile. You can eat them
hot, with spaghetti and a tomato pasta sauce, or cold
between a couple of slabs of fresh bread.

2 bread slices, crusts removed
1 kg beef mince
1 onion, finely chopped
2 garlic cloves, crushed
1 carrot, grated

2 eggs, lightly beaten
$1/2$ teaspoon each of salt and pepper
$1/4$ cup (60 ml) BBQ sauce
1 cup (150 g) plain flour
2 tablespoons olive oil

Place the bread into a food processor and process briefly to make fresh
breadcrumbs. Place the crumbs, mince, onion, garlic, carrot, eggs and salt
and pepper into a bowl and use your hands to mix well.

Roll heaped tablespoons of the mixture into balls. Put the flour into a
plastic bag, then add the meatballs and jiggle around to coat in the flour.
Shake off excess flour.

Heat the oil in a large, heavy based frying pan. Cook in 2 batches over
medium heat for 10 minutes, until well browned and cooked through.
Return the first batch to the pan to warm through.

MAKES ABOUT 40

THE PHANTOM

The 2005 Ashes series was over. Australia was in mourning for our loss as the Ashes passed back to England. It was also a tough time for Damien Martyn and me. The word on the street was that we were definitely in trouble. The fifth Test could have been my last, although I had made a century and the executioner might have given me a reprieve, but Marto's neck was in a noose and the hood had been pulled and secured firmly over his head.

Decision time! Go home and be ambushed by the press, or stay on in London in a city we all loved, particularly Kell (who was with me at the time) and Marto. If we were to go out, the all-round decision was to go out with a bang.

Now, unbeknown to us, Punter had hatched a plan with our hotel's reliable concierge. When I hailed an old black cab from outside our hotel, suddenly there was a tap on my shoulder. 'Mr Hayden, I think you have a car booked, sir,' said the concierge politely, as he prevented us from getting into the taxi.

'Er, no, mate, I don't think so. Perhaps you have the wrong name, but thanks anyway.'

'No, the car is definitely yours, sir. It has been organised for you by Mr Ponting,' he insisted.

'Really? Where to?'

'I just have to make a call, sir,' he said as stepped back inside the hotel. When he returned, he nodded his head, saying, 'It's just around the corner, sir. Have a good night, Mr Hayden!' The concierge smiled knowingly as he looked at our surprised faces.

Well, you could have knocked us all over with a feather. Bingo! There it was – a Rolls-Royce Phantom! We were looking at one million Australian dollars!

Punter had organised for us to be taken in style to Zuma, one of London's top ten Japanese restaurants. And who did we meet when we got there? None other than Ainsley Harriott, celebrity chef and the host of the *Ready Steady Cook* show in England. He is a larger-than-life character and he loves cricket. Awesome!

The other surprise of the night was when most of the England team arrived at the restaurant. That day they'd had huge celebrations in Trafalgar Square plus a ticker-tape parade. They were England's heroes and, believe you me, they were definitely in a good mood, having been celebrating for 48 hours and still going! I shouted Matthew Hoggard (Hoggy) and Michael Vaughan a beer and, although we had been fiercely competitive throughout the Ashes, here we all were, together, in a wonderful spirit of comradeship.

'The concierge smiled knowingly as he looked at our surprised faces'

Hoggy was quite funny that night. He eyeballed me and said, in true English fashion: 'Aw…to be honest, I thought you were a righteous, arrogant twat. A real cocky (whatever)!' In different circumstances, these would have been fighting words but, surrounded by good food and wine, they were funny. 'But, now…' he mumbled on.

'What?' I asked. 'Now that you've won, mate?'

'I think you're…you're a real good bloke. I …I think you're alright.'

Well, I don't know about you, but I'm in real trouble when the opposition says a bloke is alright after he's lost!

I had given Vaughan his fair share of grief and had also copped it back, I might add. Even for a fella who had been partying hard for 48 hours, it was obvious why he was the captain and, by this time, a national treasure. He's a responsible, well-mannered, even-natured bloke who has won the heart of his nation.

In the heat of the battle, no one likes to get too close to the opposition. It's best to keep them at arm's length. It's certainly hard for me to think someone is a great bloke and then have to go out the next day and belt his self-esteem and ego to billy-o! It's more important for me to find my feet with those on my own team and, when possible, invest in quality time with them.

On that night we couldn't avoid facing up to our loss, with the England team celebrating right before our eyes. The fact is, England retained the Ashes, and to be a great winner you also have to be a good loser. It was our last night in England and, for us all, it was a great memory. That Rolls-Royce Phantom was just the start.

SHABU-SHABU

You will need a table top cooker or clay pot with a burner
underneath, as the cooking is done at the table. If you are keen,
check out Asian supermarkets or specialty shops. I bought
some of these back from my tour to Sri Lanka. An electric wok
or frypan would do at a pinch. Ask your butcher about the best
quality beef cut to use, and he may even slice it for you.

750 g beef fillet
1/4 small savoy cabbage, shredded
350 g tofu, cubed
150 g fresh shiitake mushrooms, halved if large

1 cup (75 g) bean sprouts
30 g kombu seaweed
8 cups (2L) veal or chicken stock
ponzu sauce or chilli soy sauce, to serve

Cut the beef into paper-thin slices. Arrange the beef slices, cabbage, tofu,
mushrooms and bean sprouts onto a tray. Combine the kombu and stock
in the heating vessel of your choice, and bring to a simmer.

Each diner takes some of the food in their chopsticks, and dips it in the
simmering stock briefly to cook. They then transfer it to their own bowls.
To eat, dip cooked food into the sauce of your choice. The leftover stock is
served as a soup at the end.

SERVES 6

NOTE

If you part-freeze the beef fillet first, you'll find it easier to slice thinly

UNACCUSTOMED AS I AM

'I really enjoy speaking in public, especially at boardroom dinners'

Professional cricketers need to be able to speak in public, to groups of people large and small. Because of our profiles, we can help build good relationships between key sponsors and Cricket Australia, which means we have to be good communicators. It's a skill that also helps us get our own personal endorsements. I really enjoy speaking in public, particularly at boardroom dinners. I like the intimacy, as usually only about 10 or 15 people from various departments of the company attend. It can be great fun and we can hurl all kinds of shots at each other. It's interactive and competitive and provides a unique environment in which it's easy to mix one on one and listen to extraordinary people talking about their lives and businesses. It also gives me the chance to tell some of my own stories and recount the lessons I have learnt during my career.

I remember one particular boardroom dinner just after I had made 380 in a Test match. The blokes definitely went all out to be competitive.

'We can beat you, mate!'

I said: 'Beat me at what? I don't see anyone in here in whites.'

Well, unfortunately, every dog has its day. They did beat me! They gathered a group of individuals who, together, had given more than 380 years of service to their company. The group included the CEO, state managers, promotional managers, advertising managers and so on. Great service!

Then they asked me to speak. What could I do but concede defeat to 12 smart executives, all looking very wise with half-glasses perched on the ends of their noses? They had me. No way, though, was I going to let them off the hook. After all, they did hold the home advantage!

'Listen!' I said. 'You did beat me but, in my yielding, I have a request. I reckon it's only fair for each of you blokes to stand up and tell me a few yarns.'

Each of the men recounted some fantastic stories, but one tale in particular stood head and shoulders above the rest. This man told us that for two years the company had supported him while his child was dying. The great lesson I learnt from this was that of all the resources a big company has, its priority must remain with its people. I found his story inspirational, and was particularly moved by his loyalty to the company, and theirs to him. And I believe parallels can be drawn with my own career. If it wasn't for the simple loyalty of Stephen Waugh in the past and Ricky Ponting in the present, nothing I have achieved in the past decade would have been even remotely possible. They will remain significant in my life while I play cricket and in my life after cricket.

TASTY RIB-EYE WITH BEETROOT RELISH

MARINADE

4 garlic cloves, chopped

1 red chilli, chopped

1 onion, chopped

4 tablespoons olive oil

salt and pepper, to taste

4 rib-eye steaks, about 3 cm thick

8 small beetroot, stalks trimmed

$^1/_4$ cup (75 g) horseradish

12 stalks silverbeet

1 teaspoon butter

$^1/_2$ cup (125 ml) vegetable stock

Combine the marinade ingredients. Place the steaks into a shallow non-metallic dish, and pour the marinade over. Marinate for up to 1 hour, turning once.

Cook the whole, unpeeled beetroot in a large pan of boiling water for about 20 minutes, until soft. Cool slightly, then slip the skins off and trim away the tops. Place into a food processor and process until pureed. Add the horseradish cream and mix well.

Tear the silverbeet leaves from the stems and roughly chop. Heat the butter in a pan and cook the silverbeet until wilted. Keep warm.

Cook the steaks in a heavy based frying pan for 3 minutes each side over medium high heat for medium rare. Set aside to rest, and add the stock to the pan and stir to take up the pan juices.

To serve, make a bed of silverbeet, place a steak on top and add a dollop of the beetroot relish. Drizzle the pan juices over the meat.

SERVES 4

CAMPSITE DELIGHT

How much fun is it to sit around a campfire with kids and toast marshmallows? Grace just adores it. I love the outdoor life and the great thing is my kids do as well. Even little Josh, who has started walking now, enjoys being outside.

I reckon there are three wonderful things about a campsite:

- Fire. For some unknown reason, like a lot of blokes I have always had a strange infatuation with fire. I think there is something that opens up in your soul when you look into a fire and see the flames dancing and flickering in the night. Even its colours of orange, red and black fascinate me as they fuse together, change and grow brighter, then dimmer, and eventually fade to the burnt-out colours of charcoal.
- Toasting marshmallows.
- Camp ovens. The incredible ways you can control temperature and cook in them.

'I love the outdoor life, and the great thing is my kids do as well'

As a father, I believe there are so many simple lessons that can be taught to children at a campsite. For example, gathering timber to light the fire: it's important to gather just the right type of wood. It can't be too wet and it can't be too frail, otherwise it just ashes and blows away with the slightest breeze. How to be a hunter and gatherer. It's a bit like catching fish, really! There's something almost primitive about it, catching a fish and then preparing a meal on the open flame. Terrific! And it's also a great opportunity to teach kids about fire safety.

There's no better place to do these things than the beautiful Blue Lake on Straddie. It's a superb waterhole for swimming or for simply sitting around a

campfire with family and friends, eating a delicious meal, relaxing and contemplating life.

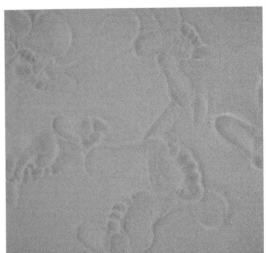

CRUMBED VEAL BAKE

This is a legendary dish around the campfire, with hot damper
or a loaf of fresh bread to dunk into the sauce.

2 tablespoons olive oil
2 onions, finely chopped
2 garlic cloves, finely chopped
2 red chillies, finely chopped
500 g ripe tomatoes, chopped
$1/2$ cup kalamata olives, pitted

salt and pepper
4 eggs
1 kg thin veal steaks (as for schnitzel),
   halved crossways
2 cups (200 g) packaged breadcrumbs
$1/4$ cup (60 ml) olive oil, extra
1 cup (125 g) grated cheese
$1/2$ cup chopped flat leaf parsley

Heat the oil in a large saucepan and cook the onion and garlic until lightly
browned. Add the chilli, tomatoes and olives, and cook, covered, on low
heat for 1 hour. Season with salt and pepper to taste.

Beat the eggs in a large bowl. Working one at a time, dip the veal into the
egg then into the breadcrumbs to coat. Heat the extra oil in a large frying
pan, and cook the veal in batches over medium heat, until browned.

Layer cooked veal and the sauce into a camp oven and top with grated
cheese. Cover and stand at the side of your fire on a low heat. Heap hot
coals onto the camp oven lid. Leave for 10-15 minutes to melt and brown
the cheese. Uncover and top with parsley.

SERVES 6

NOTE

You can also cook this in a casserole dish in the oven, at 180c for about 15 minutes

INCREDIBLE

INDIA

'Unexpected
things always
happen in India'

In many ways, the Travelex tour of India in 2004 was the Everest that Australian cricket had to conquer. Australia had mastered everyone and everything in world cricket, with the exception of beating India on their home soil. We won the four-Test series 2-1 on what was the most enjoyable tour I have been involved in throughout the years. I mark my achievements by series wins rather than personal records. That tour to India is a classic example. In 2001, I had a blistering series against India and that tour reached incredible heights for me. But, while I wasn't as successful personally on the 2004 tour, the result, the way I felt I had contributed to the win, and the way our group had gelled all helped make it the absolute highlight of my cricketing career so far.

Unexpected things always happen in India. Whether it is the crowds at press conferences or at the hotel, or the different smells and sights, there's always something going on! There's a buzz in India because of the sheer size of the population.

One of the things I enjoyed most in the 2004 series was that it was split into two parts. The first and second Tests were back-to-back and then we had eight days off before the third and fourth Tests. During the break, I had the chance to fulfil some of my ambitions to travel in India. I set off with my good friend Jacob Cherian, an Indian who has been living in Australia for the past 20 years.

I had some incredible experiences. One of these was staying on a houseboat and cruising the backwaters of Kerala. They have an amazing way of life on the waterways. The only way people can get around is by boat. They travel to school by boat. They travel to church by boat. They get their food from the waters. Despite the difficulties conditions they face in their daily lives, Kerala boasts the highest literacy rate in the world. Incredible!

Some of the photos I took on that trip say it all. I'm no photographer but I'm pretty happy with the cricket photo on the left here as, for me, it very much sums up the whole Kerala area. The Indians absolutely love cricket and in this area the kids were playing on this little strip – a patch of land ahead of a waterway, with rice paddies in the background and, to top it all off, a cow standing at fine-leg! It just tickled me.

Rice is the main source of income for the area and the paddies contribute to the beautiful scenery, awash with meandering canals as far as the eye can see. Visions of scenic north Queensland flashed into my mind as I quickly replaced the rice fields with cane fields. Frequented by Bollywood (India's version of Hollywood) movie stars, the luxury houseboats, with their air-conditioned rooms, cooks, staff and servants, were something else!

A second incredible experience was going up into the mountains where Jacob's family owned a 3,000-hectare tea plantation. Perhaps as a result of the area's colonial past, the homes of the wealthiest people are situated on beautiful hills. These overlook scattered small communities and the views are superb. Traditions are still strong and there is a timeless quality to the scene of women picking the leaves and carefully placing them into their baskets. Compared to the incredibly hot locations where we played cricket in India, the climate was cool, a real respite from the heat. The thin mountain air was just what the doctor ordered.

The food was cooked in Kerala's traditional style. It was eaten traditionally, too, with the fingers. I just love eating with my fingers. It probably comes from when I was a kid and I used to pinch Mum's cooking mixture and eat it before she had a chance to cook it! In India, eating with your fingers is the best way to experience the true texture of the different curries. All curries complement each other and they all feel so different. Nothing like a bolus of curry – yum! Absolutely delicious! And there were a lot of compliments when I ate with my fingers. 'Matt, we cannot believe you, a Westerner, eating as we do!' I have always believed that 'when in Rome, do as the Romans do'. It's a great way to get that feel for a different culture.

In the lowlands, among the water canals, there were fish curries. Prawn curries, too, were very popular. In the mountains, we were under instruction from an Ayurvedic masseur to eat a lot of fresh vegetables. Ayurveda is a philosophy of staying healthy through certain types of massage and eating well.

I love India – the people, the food, the places. And I'm really proud of the my role as a sports patron to the Global Public School in Kerala. I also love the fact that we in the Australian cricket team were finally able to climb our Everest, proudly hoist the Australian flag and say we had conquered the last frontier, India in India.

VEGETABLE PAKORA

You will need to go to an Indian specialty shop to get ajwain; if you can't then leave it out. Besan (chickpea flour) is available from health food shops.

200 g besan (chickpea flour)
$1/4$ teaspoon baking powder
2 teaspoons red chilli powder
2 teaspoons ground turmeric
2 teaspoons ajwain (bishop weed)
$1 1/2$ teaspoons cumin seeds

salt, to taste
1 cup (250 ml) water
vegetable oil, to deep fry
1 potato, peeled and thinly sliced
1 capsicum, sliced
1 eggplant, sliced
1 onion, sliced
spicy tomato or green chilli sauce, to serve

Combine the besan, baking powder, spices and salt in a bowl, and make a well in the centre. Gradually add the water, stirring to make a batter.

Half fill a large saucepan with vegetable oil. Heat over medium high temperature. Dip the vegetables into the batter, and fry a few at a time until crisp and golden. Drain on paper towels, and serve immediately with the sauce of your choice.

SERVES 4-6

VEGETABLE PARATHA ROLL

Chat masala is a spice mixture available from Indian specialty
shops. Just leave it out if you can't get it.

500 g plain flour

good pinch salt

2 teaspoons oil

300 ml water

Ghee, to cook

50 g beans, finely chopped

50 g carrot, finely chopped

50 g cauliflower, finely chopped

50 g cabbage, finely chopped

20 g butter or ghee

$^3/_4$ teaspoon cumin seeds

1 onion, chopped

30 g red capsicum, chopped

20 g tomato, chopped

1$^1/_4$ teaspoons ground cumin

1$^1/_4$ teaspoons red chilli powder

$^3/_4$ teaspoon chat masala

1 tablespoon chopped coriander leaves

Put the flour into a large mixing bowl, add the salt. Add the oil and
enough of the water to make a dough. Knead gently just until smooth.
Cover and set aside to rest.

Steam the beans, carrots, cauliflower and cabbage until just tender.

Melt the butter in a frying pan, and add the cumin seeds. When they
begin to pop, add the onion and cook until translucent. Add the capsicum
and cook for 10 seconds, then add the chopped tomato and cook for
15 seconds. Add the cooked vegetables and cook for 10 seconds. Stir in
the ground cumin, chilli powder, chat masala and coriander leaves.
Season with salt and mix well. Remove from heat.

Divide the dough into 5 portions. Roll out to a 23 cm round. Lightly
grease a heavy based frying pan and cook the paratha one at a time for
2 minutes on each side, until golden brown. Roll the vegetable mixture in
the paratha, and serve immediately.

SERVES 5

BONDAS

You will need to go to an Indian specialty shop to get urad dal and asafoetida. If that isn't possible then leave them out. Besan (chickpea flour) is available from health food shops.

2 tablespoons oil
1 teaspoon mustard seeds
1 teaspoon urad dal
2 onions, sliced
4-5 green chillies, sliced
1 kg potatoes, cooked and mashed
salt, to taste

500 g besan (chickpea flour)
1-2 teaspoons red chilli powder, to taste
pinch baking powder
pinch asafoetida (optional)
salt to taste
2 cups (500 ml) water
vegetable oil, to deep fry
chutney or tomato relish, to serve

Heat the oil in a frying pan, and add the mustard seeds and urad dal. When the seeds begin to pop, add the onion and chillies and cook for a few minutes, until soft and lightly golden. Add the mashed potatoes, and salt to taste. Mix well and remove from the heat. Cool, then roll level tablespoons of mixture into small firm balls.

Combine the besan, chilli powder, baking powder, asafoetida and salt in a large mixing bowl. Make a well in the centre and gradually add the water, mixing to make a smooth batter.

Half fill a large saucepan with vegetable oil. Heat over medium high temperature. Dip the balls into the batter and fry a few at a time until golden brown. Drain on paper towels and serve immediately with chutney or tomato relish.

SERVES 6-8

1 medium potato, peeled and thickly sliced

375 g green beans, trimmed and halved

2 carrots, peeled and thickly sliced

200 g green peas (fresh or frozen)

1 1/2 tablespoons oil

2 green chillies, chopped

1/2 cup (85 g) grated fresh coconut

1 1/2 cups (375 g) plain yoghurt

salt, to taste

Boil the potatoes, beans, carrots and peas until tender but still a little crunchy. Drain well.

Heat the oil in a frying pan and add the chillies, coconut and the vegetables. Whisk the yoghurt with salt to taste, and add to the pan. Mix gently and cook over low heat until warmed through. Do not boil.

Serve warm, at room temperature or cold.

SERVES 4

CHICKEN TIKKA

500 g chicken thigh fillets
2 tablespoons thick plain yoghurt
1 tablespoon garlic paste
1 tablespoon ginger paste

2 teaspoons red chilli powder
2 teaspoons ground cumin
1 teaspoon garam masala
2 teaspoons lemon juice
good pinch of salt

Trim excess fat from the chicken, and cut into 3 cm cubes. Place into a ceramic or glass dish.

Combine the remaining ingredients, add to the chicken and turn to coat well. Cover with plastic wrap and refrigerate for at least 2 hours, or overnight.

Soak eight 20 cm bamboo skewers in water for 20 minutes. Heat a BBQ or chargrill until moderately hot. Thread the chicken onto the skewers. Cook for 12 minutes, turning occasionally to cook evenly.

SERVES 4

HARD TO BE HUMBLE

'I never thought I'd see the Queensland flag hoisted proudly in the heart of "cockroach country"!'

I may never be invited back to the Channel 9 box but I certainly made the most of a great opportunity. I am surprised Joey Johns – all-time great rugby league superstar – could turn out to play for his club against Parramatta on the weekend following the third and deciding State of Origin game because every time a Queensland player touched the ball I belted him (not literally, of course!). He is a great fella, just unfortunate to be born south of the border! The verbal spray I gave everybody with a Blues connection left me hoarse for three days. Oh what a night! It certainly is hard to be humble when you are a Maroon.

The NRL did Queensland a huge favour holding this all-important 'grudge' match in AFL territory, and the Queensland side lapped up the support of the Melbourne crowd who in no way disguised their dislike for the Sydneysiders. Telstra Dome may not be Suncorp Stadium, but Darren Lockyer didn't seem to notice as he swooped on the ball like a seagull onto a hot chip to put Queensland in under the posts and make the result just a formality. Winning the last World Cricket Cup was sensational but seeing the Origin Shield come home to Queenland in 2006 is certainly way up there.

Because I spend so much time away playing cricket, I enjoy the simple things about being at home. Things like taking the kids to swimming lessons, tinkering with the boat, even getting the groceries from the local shops. One of my greatest passions, though, is watching footy. I am a massive Broncos fan but I am an even greater Queensland supporter come State of Origin time. It is probably fair to say I am as parochial as Gus Gould, Peter Sterling, Ricky Stuart and Laurie Daley combined. Hell, that is saying something!

Ask me to watch cricket when I am not playing and I would really struggle to sit still because I just want to be out there in the middle of it, but football has me totally rapt for the full 80 minutes. I am so into Origin that in the week leading into the games I do Sean Hampstead impersonations, complete with pretend whistle firmly clamped between my teeth and I tackle any hapless visitor who enters our home. I simply love it, whether it is watching in the lounge room at home with my family and friends, or going to the match, which I was fortunate to be able to do for the third game in Melbourne.

I've seen alot of things on Sydney's Harbour Bridge, from tourists climbing it like hungry ants to the magnificent New Year's Eve firework displays, but I never thought I'd see the Queensland flag hoisted proudly in the heart of 'cockroach country'. Oh, how sweet it was!

THE HEAT
IS ON!

When you talk about heat in a cookbook, it is usually associated with the temperature of the oven. But in this story heat refers to the pressure all Australian batsmen come under when they don't consistently score runs. The reality is that cricket is about performance. And when you are not performing, you need to look over your shoulder.

However, there's an element of 'doing it your own way' and of 'sticking to your own game' that ultimately lays the foundation of your performance. In my experience, every time I've got into trouble it's generally when I have been trying to prove someone wrong, or when I've tried to change my game to be like someone else's. Don't get me wrong, I would love to have been like Steve Waugh! His game was flamboyant through the covers, stylishly played, but the reality is I'm *not* like him. I play the way I play and the greater attention I pay to the detail of sticking to that, the better I perform.

I find it handy to say to myself, 'Next ball'. It doesn't matter about a ball in the past. It doesn't matter about some other future ball. It's simply the *next* ball. That raises a question of balance, I believe. When you are under pressure, you have to put things into perspective because, as a professional cricketer, there is one thing for certain: *you are going to have disappointments*. Luckily, I have had my fair share of disappointments and in those I have always seen great lessons and opportunities. I have turned those disappointments around, and focused on getting better, not bitter.

The inscription down the stringer on my surfboard says it all: 'Endless Progression'. When I look at those words, they fill me with optimism, purpose and, ultimately, balance. I try to apply this philosophy to everything I do, including my family life, cooking, surfing, fishing, and my relationships with friends, colleagues and business associates. I try to look at life from that perspective.

There are times in life, too, when you have to know when to push on politely – attack is not always the best method of defence in terms of the subtleties of relationships, but the strength of character and the inner resolve to acknowledge that perhaps someone has a point is. In the end, no one will remember the centuries you've made, the five-fors you've achieved or the catches you've taken; what they will remember is how your character was revealed in whatever it was you did – and in my case it's cricket.

3 large red onions, peeled and cut into thin
  wedges
2 tablespoons olive oil
1 tablespoon brown sugar
2 tablespoons balsamic vinegar

salt and freshly ground black pepper
2 cups (300 g) plain flour
1 teaspoon baking powder
220 g frozen butter
6-8 tablespoons iced water
150g goat's cheese

Preheat the oven to 170C. Combine the onion, oil, sugar and vinegar in a large baking dish. Season with salt and pepper. Bake for 45 minutes, stirring once during cooking, until tender and lightly golden. Cool completely.

To make the pastry, sift the flour, baking powder and a pinch of salt into a bowl. Grate in the frozen butter and shake through the flour to coat. Add the water, mixing through with a knife until evenly combined. Gather the dough into a ball. Wrap in plastic and chill for 30 minutes.

Preheat the oven to 220C. Divide the dough into six equal portions, and roll each one out to a 15 cm round. Crumble the goat's cheese onto each pastry base, leaving a 3 cm bare border around the edge. Reserve some of the cheese. Spread the onions on top and sprinkle with the reserved cheese. Fold the pastry over to partially cover the filling.

Place on a baking tray and bake for 5 minutes, then reduce the heat to 180C and cook for a further 30 minutes, until the tarts are crisp and golden.

MAKES 6

AN UNSUNG
HERO

'In many ways
Jock changed
my life on tour'

When you have known someone for five years and worked side by side with that person for the honour of your country, you really get to know them well. This story is about Jock Campbell (with a name like that, there definitely has to be a Scotsman hanging on his family tree somewhere). Jock's a great bloke and, despite the fact he would love to have some incredibly long title after his name, I'm just going to call him our sports and fitness trainer and (very much tongue-in-cheek) bludger and official drinks waiter. I owe him a few insults, anyhow!

Now, there aren't too many people like Jock in this world. He is very committed to his work and he's one of those people who is always there for you. On one of my off seasons, he took the time to come over to Stradbroke Island, my second home, to live with us. We had about six to eight weeks off, so it was important for me to keep up a good fitness routine. It's a real bonus to have a fellow fitness bloke with whom I can train, especially someone who is a good competitor and likes to swap a few yarns. There's always laughter when Jock's around. He really helps out heaps.

Straddie has some incredible sandhills (not to mention the picturesque view at the top). Believe you me, when I've climbed a sandhill, I know whether or not I'm fit, and in some of our sessions we would climb a couple. One day, we thought we would get a little inflatable 'rubber duckie' and Kell, Jock and I would paddle over to Moreton Island and climb one of the higher and harder sandhills. Kell was extremely fit and she was always the focus of a few terse, teasing comments, especially if she completed some of the fitness feats better than Jock and me.

But that day Kell, who was usually right up with us, if not ahead of us, was lagging. Of course, the usual hecklers got on her case, saying she was soft and all the usual rubbish that comes out when you're trying to deflate someone in fun but, at the same time, increase their incentive to work harder. We found out a few days later that she hadn't been flat due to laziness but because she was pregnant with Grace!

In many ways, Jock changed my life on tour. He is such a good person, a wonderful friend and supporter, and he also genuinely cares about his athletes, not just me but everyone in the team. His work ethic is incredible, and he has a wonderful passion for life – and pasta! Because he is so fit and strong, he needs lots of food. And when he needs it, he needs it right then and there.

Jock Campbell is one of the unsung heroes of Australian cricket over the last 10 years.

SPAGHETTI ALLA DIAVOLA

Diavola, meaning devil in Italian, refers to any dish which has been enlivened with chilli and garlic. This version is fairly mild, so add more garlic and chilli to crank it up if you like.

500 g dried spaghetti
1 cup (250 ml) olive oil
2 garlic cloves, peeled and sliced

1 teaspoon diced fresh chilli, or to taste
chopped fresh flat leaf parsley, to serve
freshly grated Parmesan cheese, to serve

Bring a large pan of salted water to the boil. Add a splash of oil and cook the spaghetti according to the packet instructions.

While the pasta is cooking, heat the oil in a pan over medium heat. Add the garlic and chilli and cook for 1-2 minutes, until the garlic starts to brown slightly. Drain the pasta and toss with the garlic and chilli oil.

Season to taste, and serve sprinkled with parsley and Parmesan cheese.

SERVES 4

WHAT SHOULD I DO WITH MY EGG YOLKS?

How good was it to have such incredible feedback concerning my last book! It's a bit like cooking a really delicious meal and getting some positive comments. I received thousands of letters from those who had tested the recipes and read the stories. It was great to be able to give enjoyment to so many people.

One of the letters that was particularly interesting had a pertinent question from a young fella down in South Australia. His question concerned the Salt-Crusted Red Emperor recipe. After he had used all the whites of the eggs, he was wondering what he should do with the egg yolks that were left over. Good question! There are three things that come to mind. First, how about doing a mayonnaise? Second, why not try a garlic aioli, which is a magnificent dipping sauce that everyone loves with chips, fish or even vegetables? It's one of those simple, classic recipes to use up those egg yolks. Finally, have you thought about ice-cream? Just the thing for summer – scrumptious!

I would like to say a special thank you to the thousands of people who wrote such lovely letters and wonderful comments about the last book. That little bit of buttering-up for the chef gave me the incentive to write another book.

Thanks a million!

'Why not try a garlic aioli, a magnificent dipping sauce that everyone loves'

ROASTED GARLIC AIOLI

I find the raw garlic in traditional aioli to be overpowering, so
I like to roast the garlic, which gives it a sweet, mellow flavour.

1 whole head garlic

pinch salt

4 egg yolks

juice of half a lemon

2 1/2 cups (625 ml) olive oil

Preheat the oven to 180C. Roast the garlic for 45 minutes, until soft. Cool, then squeeze the soft pulp from each clove. Place all the ingredients except the oil into a food processor, and process to combine. With the motor running, add the oil slowly in a thin stream until it is all combined.

MAKES ABOUT 3 CUPS

CHILLI LIME AIOLI

This variation is particularly good with seafood.

2 teaspoons dry mustard

1 teaspoon salt

1/2 teaspoon white pepper

1/2 teaspoon caster sugar

3 tablespoons lime juice

1/2 teaspoon finely grated lime rind

2 red chillies, seeded and chopped

4 egg yolks

2 1/2 cups (625 ml) olive oil

Place all the ingredients except the oil into a food processor, and process to combine. With the motor running, add the oil slowly in a thin stream until it is all combined.

MAKES ABOUT 3 CUPS

OPPORTUNITY KNOCKS IN ONETANGI

After the second Test against New Zealand, the Aussie team travelled from Wellington to Auckland, where the third and final Test was to be played. We had three full days to relax and have some downtime. At a function, I had met a woman from Travelex, the Australian team's overseas tour sponsor. I told her about my interest in wine and food and she suggested the 35-minute trip to beautiful Waiheke Island in the Hauraki Gulf. Unspoilt beaches, crystal-clear water, restaurants, olive groves – it sounded like paradise. 'You've just got to go to Stoneyridge,' she advised. 'There's a vineyard there.'

So off I went with Alfie and Kaspa.

Stoneyridge is owned by a relaxed, nuggety, charismatic guy called Stephen White, who obviously loves the good life. He had the initiative to buy a 10-hectare block at Onetangi and, within four years, had established one of the best vineyards in New Zealand. He set out to produce a wine in the Bordeaux mould, and wanted his own Cabernet-based red. He now boasts one of the best reds in New Zealand. I can certainly recommend Stoneyridge Larose, a 'claret-style' red to die for!

The moment we arrived at the vineyard, Stephen set out to make us feel really welcome. As the afternoon progressed, we could see he thought it was an honour to have us there. But we thought we were the honoured ones. How good was it to be relaxing in such a beautiful place and to experience some superb hospitality, particularly when it came to food! You should have seen Kaspa get stuck into the antipasto. And our mains were absolutely scrumptious. Because of its island setting, the restaurant has oodles of fresh fish.

That night, we met the winemakers and simply sat around, talking about Stephen White's unique experiences. He is a really colourful character and I remember laughing, later that night, when someone told me it was thought that under his pen-name, Serge Blanco, he put out a newsletter about the meaning of life – that meaning was 'sailing, mountains, geckos, G-strings, islands and red wine'! Fact or fiction … who knows? It makes for a good story, though!

We stayed at the famous pub and socialised with the locals and staff at Onetangi Beach. In the morning, we woke up, walked along the beach to con Jock Campbell, our 'fitness friend' and known lover of beautiful islands, that we had made a recovery from the previous Test match.

It was good, relaxing with two mates, totally removed from the mainstream of the group and open to whatever experiences were on offer with no deadlines, no pressure. It was one of those excellent times when Kaspa, Alfie and I take the time to go away and broaden our horizons. We are amazed at the opportunities that come our way.

As for Stephen White, I reckon he is the eternal optimist. He started with nothing but a bare field. He not only knocked loudly on that door of opportunity but he turned the handle, pushed the door open and walked straight through.

'How good it was to be relaxing in such a beautiful place'

SPINACH AND CHEESE TRIANGLES

You can substitute crumbled feta for the tasty cheese if you like,
or use a combination of both.

1 bunch English spinach
2 eggs, lightly beaten

salt and freshly ground black pepper
4 sheets frozen puff pastry, thawed
1 1/2 cups (185 g) grated tasty cheese

Preheat the oven to 200C. Tear the stems from the spinach and discard.
Wash and dry the leaves. Finely shred the leaves, and combine in a bowl
with the eggs. Season with salt and pepper.

Cut each pastry sheet into four squares. Pile a little of the spinach mixture
onto the pastry and sprinkle with cheese. Fold over to make a small
triangle. Press with a fork to seal the edge, and prick a couple of holes in
the top.

Place onto a baking tray and bake for 10-15 minutes, until golden brown.

MAKES 16

A CRICKETING CHRISTMAS

'What are you up to for Christmas?' It's a question often asked of me. Christmas for me is unique. It is so different from normal family celebrations, simply because it's like picking up home life and recreating it in a city that is on the eve of celebrating one of the biggest Australian sporting events of the calendar year – the Boxing Day Test. It is unique because I don't travel home to those I love and join in the festivities with them, they travel to where I am – Melbourne, a city that is bursting with excitement, a city that is decked out in its best Christmas colours and buzzing with the anticipation of a well-planned, iconic sporting event.

So, what was different this particular year from the last? First, we were playing South Africa in the second Test. Second, we had been beaten in the Ashes series and there was speculation aplenty about the make-up of the team. Third, Alfie was injured and I had a new opening partner in Phil Jaques. And last but not least, the MCG had undergone an incredible revamp and was now one of the best sporting facilities in the world.

'What actually happens on Christmas Day for you blokes?' This is another of those regular queries. Usually, there's the team's preparation and meeting any new players. That Christmas, we all went to the ground for a hit and I familiarised myself with the environment. It's good for me to sit on the pitch and imagine what the stadium, filled with spectators, is going to be like on Boxing Day. Meeting Phil, my new opening partner, was important too: he was out of his comfort zone and I wanted to bridge that gap and settle some of his nerves. But that's another story.

> 'I don't travel home to those I love, they travel to where I am'

Fitting Christmas in and around the Test match is always good. Because it was the only day of the year that Kell, Grace, Josh, Mum and Dad got to be with me in the middle, it was special. It was so good to see them on the same ground that I would be playing on the next day, and then to see the shenanigans of big Merv Hughes tackling Kell and tossing her over his shoulder and Gracey playing catch with Ricky Ponting as his wife Rianna looked on, laughing. Incidentally, I loved a photo of that moment so much it sat in my dressing room for the whole Test. Christmas – a time for kids? It's not bad for big kids, either!

GRANDMA'S CHRISTMAS PUDDING

2 teaspoons baking powder

1 cup (250 ml) milk

185 g butter, melted

3/4 cup (175 g) brown sugar

2 eggs, lightly beaten

3 tablespoons marmalade

2 1/2 cups (375 g) plain flour

1/2 teaspoon each ground nutmeg, allspice and
  cinnamon

375 g packet mixed dried fruit

3/4 cup (120 g) chopped dates

1/2 cup (70 g) chopped macadamias

6-8 pieces glace ginger, chopped

8 glace cherries, halved

1 cup (250 ml) rum

Dissolve the baking powder in the milk. Combine all the ingredients in a large bowl and mix until combined. Cover with plastic wrap and refrigerate overnight.

The next day, taste a little bit of the mixture and add more rum or spice if you like.

Grease a 2 litre capacity pudding bowl. Put the mixture into the bowl, and cover with a sheet of greaseproof or baking paper, and a sheet of foil. Tie securely under the rim of the bowl with a doubled length of kitchen string.

Stand the bowl on a wire rack or trivet in a large stockpot. Pour in enough boiling water to come 2/3 of the way up the bowl. Cover the pot and boil for 3 hours, topping up the water if necessary. Cool, then refrigerate until Christmas Day.

To reheat the pudding, boil the same way for 1 hour.

SERVES 8-10

HALLOWED

GROUND

My son Joshua's first experience of a Test match was in London, at Lord's, the home of cricket. Any opportunity a cricketer gets to play on that hallowed turf is to be grasped in both hands and regarded as the highlight of his career. I can remember driving down from Manchester in 1991 just to see Lord's. Middlesex were playing a home game but there weren't many people there so it was possible to get a feel for the ground, for the Marylebone Cricket Club and for the training facilities. I could tell that despite being a cricketer, as a walk-up punter there was absolutely no way I would be able to go anywhere close to the ground. Even the thought of stepping a foot on it would be enough for the 'wallopers' with their big black caps on to come round and push me into the back of the divvy van!

Lord's is a cricket oval patronised by power 'players', be they political, social or religious. It's the meeting place of a hotchpotch of socialites and iconic figures. I recall a Test match I played there before the 2005 Ashes and Queen Elizabeth II shook our hands. Our own prime minister, John Howard, has made the trek there, too. Prime ministers from all around the globe attended the first Test of the 2005 Ashes. But what made it so special for me was that Joshy, Grace and Kell came, as well as our friends Seb and Bart Wilson. Some readers may recall from my previous book that Bart was pageboy at our wedding. Well, at the end of the Test, they were all in the change room to celebrate our first win against England, who we absolutely hammered.

We really rubbed it into the Poms, too. Strains of the Aussie team's song could be heard coming from the change room. We marched across the gallows, as it were, into enemy territory and really drove it into them! England had not won a Lord's Test match for a long time and, in that moment, we were the victors and we sung and celebrated into the night. Maybe the gods of cricket looked down and snarled at us, because it was the last game we won during that Ashes tour.

Previously, in 2001, we had been encouraged to get out of the ground as soon as the match had ended. I remember writing in my newspaper article at the time that even a seagull was chased off the bloody ground! But in 2005, I had my children, especially Grace, as Josh was still a baby, playing around with Harry Gilchrist and Holly and James McGrath. There they were, running on the wicket, running on the covers, playing on all the tractors. The background was the Lord's pavilion, and we had won the Test, so it was a privileged moment to have my children out on the ground with all the other members of our family. Just unbelievable!

'Maybe the gods of cricket looked down and snarled at us, because it was the last game we won during that Ashes tour'

A picture tells a thousand words. Josh will never remember that significant Test match but Kelly, Grace and I will, and, I guess, that's how memories live on. There will be photos to say he was there. He will be proud and, even if he grows up to hate cricket, he will still understand one day, when he has the wonderful opportunity to travel overseas, just how lucky he was to be able to run around the ground, to look through the Long Room and the Lord's change room, to stand on the balcony and hear the ovation for the Australian team.

Yes, there is something almost bordering on the sacred about Lord's.

TREACLE SPONGE PUDDINGS

No wonder we haven't been beaten at the Lord's
Test match in 20-odd years.

1 cup (150 g) plain flour
2 teaspoons baking powder
$1/4$ cup (55 g) caster sugar
pinch salt

$1/2$ cup (125 ml) milk
40 g butter, melted
1 egg
few drops vanilla essence
$3/4$ cup (185 ml) golden syrup
1 cup (250 ml) boiling water
hot custard, to serve

Preheat the oven to 180C and grease six $3/4$ cup ovenproof dishes.

Sift the flour, baking powder, sugar and salt into a bowl. Combine the
milk, butter, egg and vanilla in a jug (whisk with a fork to break up the
egg), then add to the dry ingredients and gently mix until just combined.

Divide evenly between the dishes, and stand on a large oven tray.

Spoon a small amount of golden syrup carefully over the batter. Very
gently pour boiling water over the mixture. Take your time so you don't
disturb the mixture too much. It all looks a bit strange at this stage, but it
does work! Bake for 15-20 minutes until risen and firm to a gentle touch.

Stand for 5 minutes, then turn out the puddings onto serving plates
(use a folded dry tea towel to hold the dishes – they will be hot).
Serve with custard.

SERVES 6

LEMONADE SCONES FOR THE DOCTOR

When I came back from India in the summer of 2004, I felt really ill. I hadn't been well for a while before that. Even in India I had a cough, and I'd had the flu on and off for a long time. My health went downhill daily. The Boxing Day Test against New Zealand in Melbourne came and I was cooked! I was just so ill and was becoming sicker by the day. After a full night's sleep, I'd wake up feeling more tired than when I went to bed. It wasn't a joking matter, I can tell you.

I was dropped from the one-dayers, which was a godsend at the time because I simply couldn't function, and was sent to a lung specialist, Andrew Scott. Scans revealed I had pneumonia and pleurisy. If it hadn't been for Andrew, there was absolutely no way I would have got better, and when I was reselected to go to New Zealand and I scored a century in the first one-dayer, following up with a good 80, it was really on the back of his work. I was definitely improving.

Many assistants at Andrew's clinic had read my previous cookbook, and I promised to make them something when I next had an appointment. As it turned out, I had to go back to see Andrew almost one year to the day after my last appointment, so the pressure was on to fulfil my promise.

On the morning of the appointment, with Joshy on my hip, I made some lemonade scones. It was heaps of fun, and by the time we finished, Josh looked something like a rat out of a flour bin! I didn't dare tell his mother I had given him a scone for breakfast or that he had been licking the wooden spoon. The Boys' Club starts early, you know!

I arrived at the clinic with a lemonade scone, which actually looked more like a lemonade damper. It was too hard cutting out scones with little Josh all over the kitchen bench, so I hadn't bothered to make individual ones. The scone was served with honey from our very own beehive and some of Dad's homemade gooseberry jam.

'I didn't dare tell Kell that Josh had been licking the wooden spoon. The Boy's Club starts early, you know!'

LEMONADE SCONES

Last time I made these I had Josh balancing on my hip – it's just
that easy. Mind you, he looked like a rat out of a flour bin by
the time we finished!

4 cups (600 g) self raising flour
1 ¹/₂ teaspoons baking powder

300 ml lemonade
300 ml cream

Preheat the oven to 220C. Sift the flour and baking powder into a bowl,
then add the lemonade and cream. Mix lightly until evenly combined.

Pat out on a lightly floured surface until about 4 cm thick. Cut out 9 cm
rounds. Place onto a lightly floured oven tray and bake for 20 minutes,
until puffed and golden.

For sweet scones, add ¹/₂ cup sultanas or chopped dates and 2 tablespoons
caster sugar.

MAKES 9-10 SCONES

THE OLD SCHOOL GATE

Marist College, Ashgrove, in Brisbane, was a gateway for me. The school's motto says it all: 'Viriliter Age', which translated means 'to act manfully'.

Two things stand out in my mind about the school – city life and discipline. As a country fella, I had to leave the home I loved so much and become a boarder. Marist College meant I was living in the city, which was a really different experience. After the easy-going lifestyle in the bush, the comforts of home and the lack of discipline, I had to get used to the 'super-structure' of boarding school life – what time to study, what time to go to sleep, what time to eat, what time laundry had to be in, what time to have a shower … I could go on and on! I also had to learn how to cope with socialising in groups and to fit in with a culture that was different from home. I found many of those new things very, very confronting – but I learnt many things, not only about other people but also about myself.

I will always remember waking up on my first morning there. I was absolutely starving! (Food was always plentiful at home.) I found myself saying to anyone at all: 'Hey, mate, where's the food hall? Where's the mess?'

One boarder answered, 'Oh, no, no, no, no! It's not open till [whatever time it was]. You have to have a shower first and put on your uniform.' He and the other boarders gave me the lowdown.

'I had to learn to fit in with a culture that was different from home'

Well, I'll tell you what, I was first showered, first dressed and definitely first to reach the food hall. And there I saw, like the Holy Grail sitting on top of the table, this huge jug of milk. Well, that was gold! I loved milk, and thought: 'You beauty! This boarding school's not too bad after all.' So I helped myself. After I had drunk three or four glasses and eaten a couple of bowls of cereal, the rest of the blokes came in and sat down at the table. I discovered someone was the leader, and he was looking a little perplexed. He started measuring the remainder of the milk left in the jug, dividing out a ration (a word unfamiliar to me and my former lifestyle) of one cup to each boarder. But by the time the third cup was poured out, there was not a drop left. The boys were looking for answers. And I was sitting there as happy as a fat spider! The fact was I had tucked in to half a cow!

Well, it wasn't a particularly good start that morning. I made a bluey! But I didn't know, did I? The next day wasn't very pleasant. I had a table all to myself! I had learnt the hard way. But as time passed, I started to enjoy the culture, particularly in my senior year, Year 12. I was a little more settled and understood the system more. I also understood when to buck and when not to!

To this day, I have very fond memories of Ashgrove and always, ahead of the first club game of the year at Valley's Cricket Club oval, I go up to the school, alone, and say a little prayer in the Marist College Chapel. It's only a small, private chapel but it's right at the very heart of the school. It's a nice time, 20 or 30 minutes when I can sit and contemplate on my past years, and reflect, too, on the boy I was – that young bloke from the country, who had a wonderful opportunity, thanks to the sacrifice of his parents. That Matthew Hayden was a young, country teenager who, in some ways, probably took that opportunity for granted, but he now knows how lucky he was to have such a great 'school tie'.

When I first arrived I had to open 'the gate' of Ashgrove's Marist College. It led to another road on my journey of life when I had to close that gate and walk out into the real world. Now, I hold my head up high and remind myself, daily, of the school's wonderful motto, 'to act manfully'.

PASSIONFRUIT AND COCONUT CAKE

This big cake is great for feeding a crowd.

150 g butter

1 1/2 cups (330 g) caster sugar

4 eggs

2 cups (300 g) self raising flour

1 teaspoon baking powder

2 cups (180 g) desiccated coconut

1/2 cup (125 ml) milk

1/2 cup (125 ml) passionfruit pulp

ICING

3 cups (480 g) icing sugar

50 g softened butter

2 tablespoons passionfruit pulp

1 1/2 tablespoons hot water

Preheat the oven to 180C. Grease a 25 cm round tin with melted butter, and line the base and sides with non-stick baking paper.

Using electric beaters, beat the butter and sugar until creamy. Add the eggs one at a time, beating well in between.

Sift the flour and baking powder together, and combine with the coconut. Fold into the butter mixture in 3 batches, alternating with the combined milk and passionfruit pulp.

Pour into the cake tin, and bake for about 45 minutes, until springy to a gentle touch. Leave in the tin for 5 minutes then turn out onto a wire rack to cool.

To make the icing, beat all the ingredients together until creamy. Spread over the cooled cake.

SERVES 12

AUSTRALIAN SONS

I once heard the saying 'the strongest steel goes through the hottest fire', and its significance really hit home on our momentous visit to Gallipoli. Just before the 2005 Ashes tour, the Australian one-day team was given an insight into more courageous exploits of the Anzacs. In Villers-Bretonneux, near Amiens in France, we were proud to call ourselves 'Australian sons'. We were so privileged to be able to immerse ourselves, although too briefly, in the emotions of that once war-torn French village and to understand why there still exists a debt of honour and gratitude to those fearless, heroic Diggers.

Steve Waugh initiated the tradition of visiting battle sites of Australian war history and the tour, organised in conjunction with the Australian Army, took us to two places. First we went to the National Australian Memorial. This is an impressive memorial commemorating the 10,982 Australians who died in France and who have no known grave. We also went to the Franco-Australian Museum, housed in the roof of the Villers-Bretonneux school, which was rebuilt with the aid of funding from the State of Victoria in Australia, and money donated by Victorian schoolchildren whose fathers, numbering 1200, are buried in the Villers-Bretonneux cemetery. Sadly, there are many more names inscribed on the memorial.

Perhaps a little bit of history would be useful at this stage. The Battle of Villers-Bretonneux took place overnight from 24–25 April 1918, just three years

on from that atrocious battle at Gallipoli. German forces, using infantry tanks, captured Villers-Bretonneux from tired and war-worn British soldiers, as part of the German Spring Offensive on the Western Front. Then the Diggers brigades came to the fore and, in a daring, cleverly organised, strategic counterattack, recaptured the town in darkness, stopped the German advance and saved Amiens.

Our trip there was rushed. We arrived at Heathrow in London, tracked across by train to Lille, went straight out to the war memorial, then visited the school, had lunch at Le Kangaroo, went back to Lille that night and then left the next night, by train, back to London. So we got a snapshot of the Battle of the

Somme. Because of the time restraints, I wasn't able to become as absorbed by the significance of that hideous battle as I was by Gallipoli, when we visited there. On that visit, we had almost two full days on the peninsula, the whole of which is, in effect, a huge war memorial. It is untouched – rocky headlands, the lot. In France, life has gone on. The towns are busy. Time has not stood still. So, apart from the old, tell-tale trenches in the war-memorial sites, it was a little difficult to get that genuine feeling of war, especially as our visit took place in the height of summer. I believe this is a good thing. It is wonderful that towns in the Somme have been able to get on with life while people can still visit memorials to commemorate and say prayers for those brave soldiers who gave their lives, the supreme sacrifice, so that others might be free.

In some places we visit, there are kids who are dramatically affected by war every day of their lives. Yet in France, kids were kids! They asked for autographs and although there was a language barrier, that didn't matter. They laughed. They played. They were happy. They were free spirits. That is the legacy of our forefathers, the Anzacs. Inside the school hall is an inscription that reads, 'N'oublions jamais l'Australie'. It means, 'Let us never forget Australia'. I was overwhelmed with a tremendous sense of pride, not only for the honour and gratitude given to the Anzacs, but also to see how almost 100 years later the lives of the Villers-Bretonneux people have been affected, forever, by great Australians with great fighting spirits and great qualities.

As an Australian athlete, it's an incredibly uplifting experience to visit these places and to know the same Australian blood is running through my veins. But let me put it in perspective: we are not soldiers fighting for our country in a life-and-death situation (despite what the press said when we lost the Ashes!). We draw inspiration from the Anzacs' mateship, courage, sheer guts, determination, remarkable feats and fighting spirit under horrific, mind-boggling conditions (their battle was fought and won through the freezing winters of Europe). I just can't believe what pain … heartache … I mean, I just can't believe! We …we … don't even know! … So there's no point in kidding ourselves that we do.

I salute you, Anzacs (and all Australian forces, past and present). I, as an Australian son, rejoice and take great pride in recognising your heroic achievements.

ANZAC BISCUITS

1 cup (100 g) rolled oats
1 cup (150 g) plain flour
1 cup (220 g) caster sugar

³/₄ cup (705 g) desiccated coconut
125 g butter
1 generous tablespoon golden syrup
1¹/₂ teaspoons bicarb soda
2 tablespoons boiling water

Preheat the oven to 160C. Line baking trays with non-stick baking paper. Place the oats, flour, sugar and coconut into a large bowl and stir to combine. Melt the butter and golden syrup in a saucepan. Put the bicarb into a cup, add the boiling water and stir to dissolve. Stir into the butter mixture until frothy, then add to the dry ingredients and mix until evenly moist.

Roll level tablespoons of the mixture into balls and place onto the oven trays (you will probably have to cook them in batches). Flatten out slightly with your fingertips, and make sure you leave room for spreading. Cook for about 12 minutes, until flat and golden brown. Leave on the trays for 5 minutes, until firm, then transfer to a wire rack to cool completely. Store in an airtight container – do not eat all at once!

MAKES 36

ORDINARY HEROES

'They are the kinds of unforgettable people who leave footprints on your heart'

You don't have to travel the world to find amazing people. They're right here, in our own backyard. They are young and old, rich and poor, they come from all walks of life and work in all kinds of occupations. They live in country and city areas. As a matter of fact, you or I could be living, unknowingly, beside one of those people right now. Silently, tirelessly, effortlessly, happily, not looking for a pat on the back, they work. They help others: care for the sick, drive older people to buy groceries, take food to the poor, visit people in jail, read to the visually impaired … a million things! Usually, they have a great sense of humour, too. They are the unsung heroes of Australia. They are the kinds of unforgettable people who leave footprints on your heart.

I have come across hundreds of these amazing people in India, England, Sri Lanka and New Zealand, but I didn't have to go far to find these two true gems: a midwife and a hospital chaplain, both working in the same place, the Mater Hospital in Brisbane.

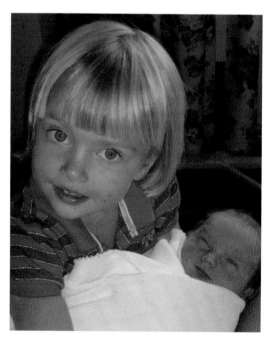

We first met Margaret, the mighty midwife, when Grace was born. The Mater Hospital encourages couples to go out to dinner about four nights after a birth. Margaret was the nursery lady, standing in the middle of all these newborn babies, and they weren't exactly as quiet as mice, either! She was completely unfazed. As she picked up a 12-pound newborn in her arms, she exclaimed, in her dry-witted manner: 'Well, just look at that! Look at that baby! No! This can't be a newborn baby. He's not a baby! He's a toddler!'

We knew Grace would be in good hands that night and when our second little blessing, Joshua Christopher, came into this world on 16 April 2005, we felt so safe and secure in the knowledge that he, too, would be in the hands of a strong, caring, lovely person who got straight to the business, someone who was a 'no dramas' person, who was completely sorted, and who would be right there for all of us. She even gave us a great recipe for cookies!

There are babies born every day at the Mater and not all of them come into the world in good health. There are some very sad cases and situations. But there is a solid rock there, a wanderer of the wards, a rugby lover and, I reckon, since he has met both sides of our family, a secret cricket fan. He is the Catholic chaplain, Father Cassian, or Cass, as he is lovingly known. What a mighty man he is! On-call 24 hours a day (no nine-to-five job for him), he rarely sleeps and is right there for everyone, whatever their faith or lack of it. He is a true treasure, has a wicked sense of humour and is an incredible storyteller. He has been a help to thousands of people and to all of our family in times of terrible grief and sadness (including the deaths of my beloved grandma, Kell's brother, Christopher, and my uncle, Father Tom Jones), unbelievably great joy (the births of Grace and Josh) and wonderful celebrations (the christening of Joshua).

When I'm home, I try to make time to visit sick kids in hospitals. What a lovely warm feeling I get when I look into their little faces and watch them light up like a Christmas tree. I reckon that's the same kind of feeling Kell's parents, Maureen and Bernie Culey, my mum and dad, Moya and Lawrie, and Kell, Grace, Josh and I have when we think of these two wonderful, unselfish human beings who work so tirelessly for others.

MELTING MOMENTS

185 g butter, softened slightly
1/2 cup (80 g) icing sugar
1 teaspoon vanilla essence
3/4 cup (115 g) plain flour
1/2 cup (75 g) cornflour

60 g unsalted butter
1 teaspoon vanilla essence
1 cup (160 g) icing sugar

Preheat the oven to 160C. Line baking trays with non-stick baking paper. Place the butter into a bowl, and sift the icing sugar over. Using electric beaters, beat until creamy. Add the vanilla and beat until combined.

Sift the flour and cornflour onto the butter mixture, and stir until combined. Roll heaped teaspoons of the mixture into balls and place onto the prepared trays. Flatten gently with a fork (dipped in flour to prevent sticking).

Bake for 15 minutes, until just pale golden. Leave on the trays for 5 minutes, until firm, then transfer to a wire rack to cool completely. Sandwich the biscuits together with butter cream, if you like.

To make the butter cream, beat the butter, vanilla and sifted icing sugar together until creamy. If you want you can flavour the butter cream with finely grated orange rind, coffee, or almond essence.

MAKES 36 OR 18 DOUBLES

WHAT A
WEEK

I guess there are many times in life when you are at a certain crossroads and, perhaps, you don't even know you are at the crossroads until you are confronted with it. There are also times when you really, really need your wife, the person who knows you best and in whom you trust the most. That was how I felt before the final Ashes Test in England.

Even though I was too proud to say I needed my wife, I *did* need my wife. But the physical distance between England and Australia just seemed too huge: there was no way I was ever going to say to Kell, 'Look, I really need you here'.

I honestly couldn't believe it when I opened the door to my hotel room at 6.30 am. I will remember it for the rest of my life. The image just blew me away.

At first there was a faint knocking, and sleepily I called out 'What?' I really didn't want to get up early that morning; I was bone tired and just rolled over in bed. The the knocking started again, more persistently this time. 'What is it?' I yelled loudly.

No answer.

A *very* loud, extremely persistent knocking started up and I thought, 'Aw, what? You have to be joking!' I shouted 'What is it?'

Even then, no answer.

So I shuffled up to the door and looked through the peephole. I saw a housekeeper. I opened the door, ready to unleash hell, especially as I had a 'do not disturb' sign on my door. Then, out of the corner of my eye, I saw little Joshy in Kell's arms. I was absolutely overcome with all kinds of emotions. What an incredibly wonderful sight.

That defined the week in a lot of ways for me. I mean, I was so euphoric that I had someone to share what was shaping up to be a really hard week. The knife was touching the heart; it was there ready to go. Kell and Josh's arrival gave me a pick-up that I can't describe. The result was that I felt such peace for the whole week in the lead up to the game, because I had my wonderful wife to share it with.

We lost the Ashes that week but, personally, I felt as though I had gained so much. First, I came through adversity and made 100 in that final Test. I saved my Test career. Secondly, I knew once again just how much sacrifice my beautiful wife was willing to make for me. And we had such an enjoyable week.

It's worth noting that lots of planets had to fall into line for our family to come together at that time. Travelling to England and then back to Australia with two young children would have been impossible. Mum and Dad and Kell's parents backed Kell all the way and had they not volunteered to have Grace, that wonderful surprise would not have eventuated. Their support was really special.

With a superb family and unbelievable support, you are the wealthiest person in the world.

BUTTERMILK PANCAKES

I absolutely love these served with maple syrup and smoky bacon. I got used to the sweet and savoury combination while on a skiing holiday in Vermont, USA. A bad habit, I know, but I figured 6 hours of skiing a day would be enough to burn these babies off!

2 cups (300 g) plain flour
2 teaspoons baking powder
1 tablespoon caster sugar
pinch salt

2 1/2 cups (625 ml) buttermilk
2 eggs, lightly beaten
80g butter, melted and cooled slightly
maple syrup, to serve

Sift the flour, baking powder, sugar and salt into a bowl. Add the combined buttermilk, eggs and butter and mix together to a smooth batter.

Lightly grease a heavy based frying pan. Pour 1/3 cupfuls of the batter into the frying pan and cook over medium heat. When bubbles appear on the top, turn over and cook the other side for 1 minute.

To make blueberry pancakes, scatter blueberries over the uncooked side before flipping.

Serve with maple syrup.

MAKES 10

LET'S HEAR IT FOR THE GIRLS!

The debate raged after the Ashes loss. Why did we lose? Why? Could it be that the players' wives and partners ('the girls') were a distraction? Articles in the press asked this question, and have prompted me to give you an insight into the life of the girls to give you an idea of how they cope on tour and around Australian venues.

Cricket Australia (CA) is possibly one of the most progressive organisations in world cricket and the Australian Cricketers' Association (ACA), the cricketing body that looks after the players, continues to develop yearly. For example, I love having my wife and family with me on tour, and CA gives the girls one overseas trip of two weeks per calendar year, for which we are extremely grateful. Although this does not finance the whole family's flight, it does pay for an extra room for the children, if required. During the visitors' period, the board also organises a minibus to transport families to the grounds. Times have changed, as have players' benefits. Even in '93, when I started my international career, wives were not allowed stay in the same hotels as the players.

The girls have to be very special people. They are away from us for many months a year and, believe you me, touring for them isn't always beer and skittles. Kell once put it simply:

'The girls have to be very special people'

The boys don't get a lot of spare time. Whatever time we get with them is worth it. Worth it for everyone – even a glimpse at breakfast! The priority is Matt when we tour so, with a young family, we get a separate room so he can have a good night's sleep. We are in this life together and there is a need to understand his job and pressures, and to be there for him to break up his busy schedule. Being with him gives a sense of reality to our children, too. They need to understand his life, what he does.

In saying that it also gives our kids an amazing flexibility. They become used to travel, and meeting new people. They become very gregarious. The children of our 'cricketing family' are like brothers and sisters and, I guess, I'm like an 'aunt' to them. It's a difficult ask for little children to watch the game all day so, when possible, the girls, with or without children, all look after each other and plan excursions. For example, Jane McGrath lived in the Cotswolds in England before marrying Glenn, and took us all to an unbelievable miniature cottage. A dinosaur museum was another great jaunt. The kids just loved these.

We are very fortunate in Australia. When we go to watch the boys, CA provides us with private boxes, where children have some roaming room and, in Melbourne and Sydney over the Christmas–New Year period, there is even a creche. No other country does this at all and, I guess, it all comes down to budget.

Sometimes it is a massive effort to even get to the grounds. In South Africa, it's not safe to jump in a taxi without security advice. It really all depends on the country. I remember, in England, when Matt was batting in the last Ashes Test, it took me two hours even to arrive at the ground and, with Josh still a baby, it was difficult. Then, at the ground, there were no facilities for us and we had to sit out in the sun. CA does provide facilities for touring wives/partners and children when they come to Australia, however. That's a really good thing for them.

I remember hearing from the boys after I had batted in Adelaide, when Kell was pregnant with Josh, that she had been thrown out of the SACA! Now, no one is more fastidious about dressing according to the standards of each ground and with her own great fashion sense than Kell. She always makes sure she checks on rules. She laughs, now, as she reminisces.

Oh, yes! How embarrassing! The girls were in a state of disbelief. I was six months pregnant with Josh and wore a long black skirt and very fashionable strapless top – certainly no bare tummy protruding. I was not allowed in! Sue Langer was with me and tried to plead my case but to no avail.

'But that's ridiculous. That's not a boob tube. What if I were to find two shoelaces and put one over each shoulder for her?' entreated Sue.

'No! No boob tubes allowed,' answered the man sternly. 'She can go and purchase a Redbacks T-shirt and use it as a top'!

Desperate, the girls found only one T-shirt left – size XXL. It would have covered all of Kell, even six months pregnant! So back to the hotel she went, changed, and walked back.

That night, the media caught a sniff of what had happened. Kell was offered a gift voucher from a maternity shop in South Australia.

The days gone by were definitely harder for the girls and players' families, and they are certainly getting better. As for being a distraction, I can assure you there is nothing like having a wonderful, supportive wife and family.

APPLE CRUMBLE

You can vary this recipe by adding fresh or
frozen berries to the apple, if you like.

800 g can bakers apple
1 teaspoon ground cinnamon
$^1/_2$ cup (90 g) sultanas
1 cup (150 g) plain flour

$^1/_2$ cup (115 g) brown sugar
$^3/_4$ cup (70 g) desiccated coconut
125 g butter, chopped
ice cream or double cream, to serve

Preheat the oven to 180C. Spread the apple into a 5 cup capacity
ovenproof dish. Sprinkle the cinnamon and sultanas over the apple.

Combine the flour, sugar and coconut in a mixing bowl. Using your
fingertips, rub the butter into the dry ingredients to make a crumbly
mixture.

Spread the crumble over the apple, and bake for 20 minutes, until brown.
Serve hot with ice cream or double cream.

SERVES 6

BLUEBERRY SURPRISE

Peter Robertson, the owner and winemaker at picturesque Brookfields vineyards and restaurant, is a long-time supporter of New Zealand cricket and he has had his fair share of touring sides visit his restaurant. After the fifth and final one-day international in New Zealand, the opportunity arose to get together with the New Zealand team and the boys jumped at it. Steve Bernard organised it. We had three spare days before we ventured up to Auckland for the start of the Test series. Luckily, for that trip I had Kell and Grace with me as well.

Brookfields is one of the oldest wineries in Hawkes Bay, and is situated between Napier and Hastings along the Tutaekuri River. Its attractive rose gardens and fine views of the vineyards make it just the right place for some quality time out.

Now, Simmo and Hoggy decided to go to the bowels of Brookfields' very impressive cellar, and returned in a slightly inebriated and jovial state. Just prior to dessert being served, Punter noticed Grace was playing with some Play-Doh on the grass.

Simmo had ordered a scrumptious-looking custard tart, served with fresh King Island cream from Tasmania and decorated with mouth-watering blueberries, which are beautiful around Hawkes Bay because the cool climate is ideal for them.

Punter had an idea. The colour of Gracey's Play-Doh was an almost-perfect match for the blueberries that garnished Simmo's dessert. He could see, too, that Grace was rolling the putty into small balls.

Hey presto! A quick replacement of blueberries with Play-Doh and the laugh was on Simmo!

'The colour of Gracey's Play-Doh was an almost-perfect match for the blueberries that garnished Simmo's dessert'

ORANGE RING CAKE

This has to be the quickest and easiest cake ever made.

60 g soft butter

1 cup (220 g) caster sugar

2 eggs

1 tablespoon orange juice

1 teaspoon finely grated orange rind

2 tablespoons milk

$^1/_2$ teaspoon vanilla essence

1 $^1/_2$ cups (225 g) self raising flour

sifted icing sugar, to decorate

Preheat the oven to 180C. Lightly grease a 20 cm ring tin and line the base with non-stick baking paper.

Place all the ingredients into a bowl, and using electric beaters mix on low speed until combined.

Increase the speed to high and beat for 2 minutes only. Pour into the tin, and bake for 30 minutes, until the cake springs back to a gentle touch. Leave to stand in the tin for 5 minutes. Run a knife around the outside and inside ring of the cake, and turn out onto a wire rack to cool.

Put some icing sugar into a small fine sieve and dust over the top of the cake before serving.

SERVES 8

THE $28 FISH

Spontaneity. A word that is soon forgotten when you have a young family and one that is quickly replaced by 'routine', as you try to stay consistent and run a steady ship. Unfortunately, or fortunately, depending on which way you look at it, the professional cricketer's nomadic lifestyle makes routine virtually impossible so I'd be lying if I said I wasn't surprised by a call I received from my wife Kellie, announcing a surprise visit while I was on tour in New Zealand.

'Matt, Gracey and I are on an 8am flight to Auckland, connecting to Napier, and arriving at 5.30pm tomorrow. What do you reckon?'

'That's great!' I responded excitedly. 'You sure you're okay to travel?'

Now, my mum and dad taught me it was rude to answer a question with a question but, in this case, I believed it was warranted. You see, Kell was expecting our second baby in just under a month. So you could excuse me for thinking things were getting tight.

'Look, I've been to the doctor today. He said that everything is going really well and it should be alright. Plus Grace and I have been really missing you and if we don't take the opportunity now, it just won't happen.'

Kell always has a way with words that puts my mind at ease. I couldn't have been any happier to hear the news that my family was on the way to see me. It had been a long few weeks of very frustrating, slow progress on my injured shoulder, suffered while taking an outfield catch in Christchurch to dismiss Chris Cairns in the second one-dayer.

One truly great advantage that a professional sporting career has over nine-to-five work is the occasional window of opportunity for downtime. Some would argue wasted time, but not this little black duck! When I do have time for my family, it is such great quality time. Kell's trip over, despite the huge effort, pretty much guaranteed hours of opportunity to have some fun. So, as soon as I hung up the phone, my mind went into action.

Napier is an almost perfect location. Situated on the tranquil east coast in the middle of the North Island is a region known as Hawkes Bay. The locals call it 'The Fruit Bowl of New Zealand', where, after the Second World War, the people of the famous Heretaunga Plains opened their arms to a thriving horticultural industry. Orchards, market gardens and vineyards abound. Yep, you guessed it – that means cellar doors and restaurants … a food and wine haven!

At training that morning, it turned out a few of us were in the same boat. Our team's massage therapist, Lucy Frostick, Kaspa and Gilly were all at loose ends that afternoon so the team bus was marked 'out of action'. We visited many beautiful locations that day, but the highlight was lunch at a vineyard called Craggy Range. It was owned by a true-blue, dinky-di Aussie who had managed to nestle his way into one of the prominent ridges of Te Mata Peak. His Craggy Range Avery Vineyard, Marlborough Riesling and Sauvignon Blanc were aptly described by Kaspa: 'Ripe melons! Passionfruit characters are just getting in the swing of it! Mmmmm! That tasted bloody good, didn't it?' Now Kaspa might be colourblind but the Big Quick from Queensland sure has his fair share of tastebuds. The wines perfectly complemented the fish dish and the day turned out to be one of the more memorable days of my life.

Steve Bernard, the Australian cricket team's manager, has many skills but none as refined as his ability to sniff out an opportunity to taste quality red wine. The boys, too, are no slouches when they sense a lull in the program or an opportunity to celebrate. So, when a note was passed under my door saying there was a team dinner at one of the local vineyards outside Napier, its location didn't come as any great surprise.

The interesting thing about this particular function was that, unknown to all of us, the New Zealand cricket team was also on the guest list. In fact, it was Stephen Fleming, New Zealand's skipper, along with his long-time friend Peter Roberston, owner and chief winemaker of the beautiful Brookfields Estate, who had organised the evening.

I love people-watching and it certainly proves very interesting when two opposing teams come together in a social situation. Kaspa, Gilly and Binga (Brett Lee) are good mixers, but the greatest 'mixer' of all was a $28 fish that was purchased and placed on the table. That fish was a great conversational piece, because it had been wood-fired and the taste was amazing. It proved to me once again that good food brings people together (even Kiwi cricketers!) in a spirit of fun and friendship.

'Great food brings people together'

157

ACKNOWLEDGEMENTS

Writing my first cookbook a couple of years ago marked the start of a new and exciting chapter in my life, one that enabled me to express my love of home cooking in the best possible way. And it has created wonderful opportunities for me to meet hundreds of people from all walks of life who have been generous enough to encourage me to publish some more of my yarns and recipes in this second book. From the lady in the elevator politely saying, 'Matt, my husband just loves your dhal curry' to the little boy who emailed baggygreen.com saying, 'Matt, Mum doesn't want to waste the egg yolks from your Salt-Crusted Red Emperor. What should we do with them?', the feedback I've received for my first book has been an absolute golden highlight for me and Kell. I'd therefore like to thank you, my readers and fellow home-cooks, for your inspiration and encouragement.

I'd also like to thank all at International Quarterback and ABC Books for giving me this fantastic opportunity to share, once again, my passion for food and telling a tale or two.

Finally, when you flick through the pages of this book, I'm sure you will see just how important and precious my whole family is to me. I'd like to thank them all for their continued love and support.

Published by ABC Books for the
AUSTRALIAN BROADCASTING CORPORATION
GPO Box 9994 Sydney NSW 2001

First published November 2006

ISBN 10: 0 7333 1993 9
ISBN 13: 978 0 7333 1993 8

*Cover photographs: Justin Levitt Photography (front cover top), Getty Images/Hamish Blair
    (front cover bottom left and bottom right), Paul A. Broben (front cover bottom centre).*
Project management: Tracy Rutherford and saso content & design
Design: saso content & design pty ltd
Food editor: Tracy Rutherford
Food photography: Andre Martin
Food stylist: Jane Collins
Additional photography see picture credits below
Set in Palatino and Today by saso content & design pty ltd
Colour reproduction by Graphic Print Group, Adelaide
Printed and bound in Singapore by Tien Wah Press

5 4 3 2 1

PICTURE CREDITS

AAP/AP PHOTO/MARK BAKER: 29, 102; ANDRE MARTIN: 10, 17, 20, 26, 27, 30, 36, 37, 40, 45, 48, 53,
58, 63, 66, 71, 74, 79, 82, 89, 90, 95, 96, 101, 104, 109, 112, 116, 120, 126, 130, 135, 138, 143, 146, 151, 154;
GETTY IMAGES/TOM SHAW: 125; GETTY IMAGES/HAMISH BLAIR: 5, 7, 47, 73, 85 cr, 85 br, 87, 92,
94 t, 94 b, 98 tl, 98 b, 107, 145; JUSTIN LEVITT PHOTOGRAPHY: 12, 13 tl, 18, 24 tl, 24 tr, 24 bl, 25 tl, 25
tr, 25 br, 33, 34 tr, 34 cr, 34 br, 34/35, 77, 111 tl, 111 tr, 111 bl, 111 br, 129; MATTHEW HAYDEN: 9, 13 tr,
13 bl, 13 br, 22, 23, 28, 32, 38, 39 tl, 39 bl, 43, 46 tl, 46 cl, 46 bl, 50, 51 tr, 51 br, 54 tl, 54 cl, 54 bl, 55 t, 55 cl,
55 c, 55 cr, 55 b, 60, 61, 69, 72, 80 t, 81 tl, 81 tr, 81 cr, 81 bl, 81 br, 84, 85 tr,98 tr, 99, 106, 114, 115, 123, 124
tl, 124 tr, 124 cr, 124 b, 132, 133, 136, 137 tr, 137 cr, 137 br, 140 bl, 140 br, 141 tr, 141 br, 148, 153, 156 tl,
156 bl, 157; NEWSPIX/BRETT COSTELLO: 65; NEWSPIX/COLLEEN PETCH: 56; NEWSPIX/LYNDON
MECHIELSON: 64, 158; NEWSPIX/MICHAEL KLEIN: 118,119; NEWSPIX/WAYNE LUDBEY: 89/87;
PAUL A. BROBEN: 14/15, 42, 80 b, 144, 159; SASO CONTENT & DESIGN: 25 bl: VINCENT LONG
PHOTOGRAPHY: 103

KEY TO LEGEND: t=top, b=bottom, c=centre, tl=top left, tr=top right, cl=centre left